Piano Music for One Hand

Piano Music for One Hand

Theodore Edel

Indiana University Press

BLOOMINGTON AND INDIANAPOLIS

*The paper used in this publication meets the minimum requirements of
American National Standard for Information Sciences—Permanence of
Paper for Printed Library Materials, ANSI Z39.48-1984.*

(∞)™

MANUFACTURED IN THE UNITED STATES OF AMERICA

Library of Congress Cataloging-in-Publication Data

Edel, Theodore, date
    Piano music for one hand / Theodore Edel.
      p.   cm.
    Includes bibliographical references.
    ISBN 0-253-31905-6 (cloth : alk. paper)
    1. Piano music (1 hand)—Bibliography.   2. Piano music (1 hand)—
History and criticism.   I. Title.
ML128.P3E3   1994
786.2'19365—dc20   94-5139

1 2 3 4 5 00 99 98 97 96 95 94   MN

CONTENTS

Preface

Few pianists suspect the true scope and size of the one-hand literature—nearly a thousand solo works for left hand, dozens of concerti, and much chamber music. At least sixty pieces exist for right hand alone. A few selections, such as the *Nocturne* by Scriabin and Ravel's *Concerto*, have received well-merited attention. But why ignore all that music which, from the viewpoint of technical development, may be more useful and at the same time constitutes an unusual facet of the repertoire? And not all left-hand music is from the Romantic era: a surprising number of works are contemporary, even avant-garde.

As I have twice experienced personally, temporary injuries can take a pianist by surprise. One night I stumbled on a pile of branches and fell on my right wrist, spraining it badly. My right hand was out of commission for a month. Several years later, when I was a few minutes into the only tennis class of my life, I ran for a long shot and took a nasty fall on the same wrist. The result: a broken navicular bone and six weeks in a cast.

Students occasionally suffer similar damage to their hands, with more or less dire results. All players, from master pianists to young aspirants—whether they will soon be able to return to the standard repertoire or never again—need to know that there is a vast body of music for them, in every style and genre, from the simplest note-stepping to the dizzy heights of pyrotechnical display.

In the catalogue entries in Part II, the emphasis is on objective data—tempo, character, texture, harmonic vocabulary, degree of difficulty, length, and publication information. Subjective value judgments are also made on musical worth and idiomatic writing for a single hand. In a list containing so much nineteenth-century salon music, it was inevitable that some of those judgments would be negative. However, I did not omit works for any reason: I considered it best to list all the material for one hand known to me and allow others to examine the music and make up their own minds. Musical examples are provided for works of musical distinction or special technical value.

Arrangements and transcriptions are listed under the arranger, not the original composer (Godowsky, not Chopin). Music for *two* hands with a difficult left-hand part—and many such works have mistakenly found their way onto lists of left-hand music—has been excluded.

Entries are as complete as possible but vary according to the data available. For certain obscure composers no biography could be found; for some works only reprints were available. And there are pieces, though known to have been printed (from Hofmeister's catalogue, etc.), which could not be located and examined. These are listed without commentary. Whenever possible, a library location for the music is given. Unless otherwise noted, translations are my own.

Because music continually goes in and out of print, there is no attempt at classifying works as being "in-print." Joseph Rezits' *Piano Music in Print* can serve as a rough guide—it has a section on available left-hand music—but that book was last issued in 1978.

A visit to the Library of Congress in Washington, D.C., will yield the fullest results: hundreds of works may be seen there and tried on the piano. There is also a fair-sized collection at the New York Public Library (Library of the Performing Arts at Lincoln Center), though it is less convenient to examine. The American Music Center (30 W. 26 St., New York, NY 10010) receives many recent American scores in manuscript. Those with access to an interlibrary loan system have at their disposal the holdings of thousands of libraries. In Europe, the great collection is at the British Library. Also in London is the Disabled Living Foundation (380–384 Harrow Road, London W9 2HU); its Music Advisory Service publishes lists of left-hand works held in libraries and those available from the Foundation itself.

This book was made possible by a sabbatical leave from the University of Illinois at Chicago. I would like to thank the library staff of the University, particularly Kathy Kilian, as well as the staff at the Library of Congress. Robert N. Levin read the original manuscript and offered many valuable suggestions. Special thanks go to my wife, Chun, for conceiving the idea of studying piano music for one hand.

Abbreviations

A number of works appear in three extensive anthologies:

"Australian" = *Piano Music for One Hand by Australian Composers*, compiled by Shirley Harris (Melbourne: Allans Music Australia Pty. Ltd., 1984).

"Lewenthal" = *Piano Music For One Hand, A Collection of Studies, Exercises and Pieces*, edited by Raymond Lewenthal (New York: G. Schirmer, 1972).

"Georgii" = *Einhändig: Eine Sammlung von originalen und übertragenen Kompositionen*, edited by Walter Georgii (Cologne: P.J. Tonger, n.d.).

Degrees of technical difficulty:
E = Easy
M-E = Moderately easy
M-D = Moderately difficult
D = Difficult

NYPL = New York Public Library at Lincoln Center
L of C = Library of Congress, Washington, D.C.
Brit. Lib. = British Library, London

Piano Music for One Hand

Part One

INTRODUCTION

1.

Survey of the Literature

The story of one-hand piano music is primarily the story of music for the *left* hand alone, in that right-hand works make up only a small percentage of the repertoire and are of more recent origin. The vast repertoire for the left hand created over the last 150 years arose from a variety of causes: technical development, injury, compositional challenge, and virtuoso display. Four players have been singled out for separate sketches. Alexander Dreyschock and Adolfo Fumagalli were pioneers, the first two pianists to perform in public with their left hands alone. The origins of left-hand music are tied to the rise of the solo piano recital, and their concerts exemplify much about European musical life in the mid-nineteenth century. In later decades the one-armed pianists Geza Zichy and Paul Wittgenstein had unique careers of great interest.

TECHNICAL DEVELOPMENT

The piano literature for two hands, in fact, the literature of all instruments, is rich in studies, or *etudes*—pieces at every level of difficulty designed to augment a player's technical skills. Similarly, one of the key purposes of left-hand music, to judge from the sheer numbers of technical works created, has been pedagogic. Because the standard piano literature favors the right hand so much, by playing that literature virtually every pianist, whether a great virtuoso or a fumbling student, eventually comes upon a crucial gap in ability: the right hand can do things that the left finds impossible. And yet the left must function with subtlety, strength and precision, and at times it is called on to perform the most difficult feats. The myriad studies for left hand alone—those which carry that title as well as those that bear other names but are really "studies"—have been largely an attempt to close this gap in skill. Sometimes the relationship was personal: Saint-Saëns created his *Six Etudes* for the students of his friend Louis Diémer, teacher at the Paris Conservatory. According to Robert Casadesus, the best one, the *Bourée,* went to him.

Every serious pianist, at some point in his or her development, must face this problem of the left hand. Although there are many two-hand works with a difficult left-hand part—Chopin's *"Revolutionary" Etude* and the Czerny *Left Hand Studies,* op. 718, are only two from a multitude of possible examples—none offers quite the same opportunity for putting the left hand "under a microscope" as music for left hand alone. It is primarily a matter of increased awareness. While some players, especially professionals, may have the maturity to adhere to high standards at all times (for example, always playing the fast running bass notes of a Beethoven concerto evenly and clearly, even when the right hand is busy with the melody), there are many more who allow the details of the left hand to get lost.

Young people in particular can benefit from this total "exposure" of the left hand. Given human nature, it is more likely that a Moszkowski *Etude* for the left hand alone will be practiced more evenly and with greater precision—creating better technical habits—than will occur when the same pianist works on Chopin's *"Revolutionary" Etude.* And since important habits are formed in the young years, careful work on the Moszkowski (though admittedly of lesser musical value) may enable a player to master the greater music later on.

There is also the question of confidence. Singing a solo before an audience would be a growth experience—even if not a totally positive one—never to be gained by participating in a vocal quartet. To master and give a decent performance of a piece for the left hand alone is to come just a little closer to believing in yourself, which may be the most valuable regimen of all.

Each of the extensive *Schools* for left hand by Berens, Bonamici, Phillip, and Wittgenstein—to list them in order of increasing difficulty—offers a complete course of left-hand training through the inclusion of exercises, studies, and transcriptions. (How strange that Czerny, with his mania for the encyclopedic, never produced a school for the left hand alone.) In our own time, with the codification of teaching material for young people, there has been an array of simple left-hand music for children.

All of this said, let us not make exaggerated claims for left-hand music. If the final goal is two-hand playing, the left hand must be fully integrated. That is, the crucial thing for a pianist is the way the left hand functions while the right is playing. A whole world of habits may be involved. Recent research in the very complex area of physical psychology indicates that the left hand may be doing something rather different when it plays by itself than when it functions with its partner.* So one-hand music should not be seen as a cure-all.

---

*According to Leon Miller, Professor of Psychology at the University of Illinois at Chicago, in bi-manual playing the brain must control what each hand does separately as well as what the hands are doing together. There may also be some "spillover" of commands from one hand to the other.

INJURY

Some pianists have no choice in the decision to study left-hand music. The number of players who have sustained serious permanent damage to their right hands through accidents, overpracticing, strain, nerve deterioration, or some other cause is tragically high. In fact, the treatment of injured performers is becoming an American industry, with a journal—*Medical Problems of Performing Artists*—and major centers in at least seventeen cities.

In the nineteenth century virtually everyone was right-handed; that is, until recently the small minority of individuals who were born left-handed were discouraged from using the left hand and forced to conform to the majority. This would presumably lead to a great preponderance of right-hand injuries sustained in daily life away from the piano. As for *playing*-related impairments, since the right hand has the most complex music and bears the burden of projecting the melody as well, the harm caused by the strain of overpracticing and by incorrect practicing generally strikes there. The classic case was Robert Schumann. Working without a teacher, the impetuous nineteen-year-old set himself an impossible regimen, which included a ten-fold repetition of his newly composed *Toccata*! After two years of trouble, Schumann sealed his fate with a contraption designed to strengthen the fourth finger of his right hand. What had begun as a sensation of numbness led to a crippling paralysis of at least two fingers.

Although Schumann's struggles bore no compositional fruit, the very first published work for the left hand may have resulted from a physical disability. In 1820 Ludwig Berger brought out his *Studies*, op. 12. Three years earlier an apoplectic stroke had rendered his right arm useless. That would explain the inclusion of one study for the left hand.

When Alexander Scriabin was a student at the Moscow Conservatory, his teacher Vassily Safonoff advised him to "sink into the keys, don't skitter over them." Scriabin (he was the same age as Schumann had been) decided to go at it with a vengeance. Determined to play Balakirev's *Islamey* and Liszt's *Don Juan Fantasy* as fast as his phenomenal classmate Josef Lhevinne, he rented a summer house and banged away at his piano day and night. The result: tendinitis of the right hand and a prediction from his doctors that he would never play again. But Scriabin refused to despair and fortunately had the good sense to totally rest his strained hand. He worked patiently with the left hand alone, although we do not know what material he played. After six months he could use his right hand again, but it would be two more anguished years before he achieved a complete recovery. The *Prelude and Nocturne*, op. 9, written two years after his problem began, were not the only fruits of this youthful crisis. From this point on, the piano music of Scriabin evinced a wonderful richness (and difficulty) in the left-hand parts (see Ex.1).

For the rest of his life, Scriabin obsessed nervously over his right hand, continually looking at it and tapping it on the table while speaking with people. Aside from the appeal of the music, might the frequent inclusion of the *Prelude and Nocturne* on his concert programs indicate a wish to rest his delicate right hand for several minutes?

EX. 1. Scriabin: *Sonata* no. 6 (Belaieff, 1912), mm. 248–249.

It seems that during the time of his injury Scriabin also devised a left-hand para-phrase on waltz themes by Johann Strauss. His friend Rozamov often heard him playing it, and wrote, "God alone could count the virtuoso tricks it contained." In 1907, Scriabin played this waltz in New York City:

> There was quite a to-do over me in America. . . . The left hand Nocturne always enjoyed a special success. Then and there I somehow remembered that I had composed a wickedly clever waltz for the left hand, after the manner of Strauss, full of virtuoso passages, octaves, and it was ghastly! I composed it so as to exercise my left hand when I was ill, and it was at a time when I was a . . . worldly person. And so I decided to play this waltz for the Americans to see what would happen. I played it and it brought the house down, could not have been better. Suddenly in the middle of this noise and applause, I heard one single, piercing hiss. . . . It seems it was an acquaintance of mine, a Russian, who happened to be in town and came to hear the concert. He was expressing his disapproval for what he thought was disgraceful for me. . . . And I too felt ashamed, and I never played that waltz again.[1]

Scriabin's *Waltz* has not been found—perhaps he never wrote it down.*

Count Geza Zichy, who made a playing career after losing his right arm in a hunt-ing accident, had a few works composed for him. They include a song transcription by his friend Franz Liszt and Emil Sauer's fine *Etude*.

We can only imagine the number of musicians who returned from the front maimed after World War I. Two of the most celebrated cases were Ottakar Hollman of Czechoslovakia, whose arm was permanently paralyzed, and the Viennese Paul Wittgenstein, who suffered an amputation. Hollman convinced two of his fellow-countrymen to compose for him—Janáček (*Capriccio for Piano and Winds*) and Martinů (*Divertimento* for piano and chamber orchestra). In addition he received a *Sonata* by Janoslaw Tomasek, one of the very few left-hand works in that genre. Wittgenstein commissioned dozens of pieces, most of them chamber works and concerti, and his great wealth ensured that many were by illustrious composers.

At the end of World War II, Walter Georgii, also with the injured in mind, com-piled a large volume of both old scores and newly commissioned works by German composers. Maria Büttner's *Austrian Dances* contains a poignant Afterword dedicating her music to the wounded soldiers.

---

*Although Scriabin and his Russian friend were so ashamed of the left-hand *Waltz*, something quite different soon scandalized the public: when it was discovered that the composer was traveling with his mis-tress, Scriabin had to make a hurried exit from New York.

In 1948, the British pianist Harriet Cohen sustained a bizarre injury: she was holding a drinking glass in her right hand when, for no apparent reason, it suddenly shattered. The damage done to her hand was too great for the continuance of her career, but she was fortunate in having as a close friend the prominent composer Arnold Bax. He wrote a *Concerto* for her.

The Dutch pianist Cor de Groot, during a period when his right hand was incapacitated (1959–60), received works from six Dutch colleagues; at the same time he composed for his own use the *Variations-Imaginaires* for left hand and orchestra. Another composer-pianist writing for himself during a brief period of right-hand injury was the American Robert Helps. Leon Fleisher and Gary Graffman are no longer able to play with their right hands, and their plight has inspired several recent compositions, including concerti by C. Curtis-Smith (for Fleisher) and Ned Rorem (for Graffman).

Because so much of the literature for left hand alone was created by composers no longer known, for each story that we do possess there are many more lost in the mists of history. Although it is not possible to reconstruct the circumstances of their creation, the dedications found on these scores may indicate the existence of an injured student or colleague.

COMPOSITIONAL CHALLENGE

In the preceding discussion of technique and injuries, the emphasis has been on the needs of performers. But left-hand music may also arise from an inner *compositional* urge. This might be the challenge to create something complete with an incomplete number of fingers or, in the case of Johannes Brahms, a special aesthetic pleasure. When Brahms played Bach's string music on the piano he felt the satisfaction of limitations—Bach had used only four strings, so Brahms would use only five fingers. Out of this activity arose his version of the *Chaconne* for violin. As he explained his experience to Clara Schumann:

> The Chaconne is in my opinion one of the most wonderful and most incomprehensible pieces of music. Using the technique adapted to a small instrument the man writes a whole world of the deepest thoughts and most powerful feelings. If I could picture myself writing, or even conceiving, such a piece, I am certain that the extreme excitement and emotional tension would have driven me mad. If one has no supremely great violinist at hand, the most exquisite of joys is probably simply to let the Chaconne ring in one's mind. But the piece certainly inspires one to occupy oneself with it somehow. One does not always want to hear music actually played, and in any case Joachim is not always there, so one tries it otherwise. But whether I try it with an orchestra or piano, the pleasure is always spoiled for me. There is only one way in which I can secure undiluted joy from the piece, though on a small and only approximate scale, and that is when I play it with the left hand alone. And then at times I cannot help thinking of Columbus' egg. The same difficulty, the nature of the technique, the rendering of the arpeggios, everything conspires to make me—feel like a violinist! Portschach, June, 1877[2]

Brahms's absolute fidelity to the original *Chaconne*, so unusual for the Romantic period, resulted from his deep reverence for Bach's music.

In any study of left-hand music, Leopold Godowsky must inevitably take pride of place, and his name will recur often in the following pages. Not only did he create the greatest number of works, but they stand alone in the piano literature as the last word in complexity, ingenuity, and technical difficulty. Pianists exploring his music for the first time will most likely have a reaction similar to that of Leon Fleisher: "I was rummaging the other day and came across a marvelous piece called *Symphonic Metamorphosis on Themes from the Gypsy Baron* by Leopold Godowsky. I can barely get through it with two hands! It's not to be believed—virtually unplayable."[3]

The heart of Godowsky's left-hand output are the *Paraphrases on Chopin's Etudes*. Of these 53 Chopin/Godowsky *Studies*, 22 are for the left hand alone. Godowsky put forward his broad compositional purpose in the Preface: "to develop the mechanical, technical and musical possibilities of pianoforte playing, to expand the peculiarly adapted nature of the instrument to polyphonic, polyrhythmic and polydynamic work, and to widen the range of its possibilities in tone coloring."

Godowsky believed that, in regard to the piano, the left hand holds a superiority over the right: 1. it has the stronger fingers placed naturally for the playing of upper voices; 2. it is more elastic by being much less used in daily life; 3. it is well positioned for playing the all-important low bass notes. Surely Godowsky was making these claims on behalf of his own left hand, for pianist William Mason called him "unapproachable in his specialty. His left hand is in every respect the equal of his right, and passages of extreme intricacy and rapidity come out with astonishing clearness of detail."[4]

More than simply offering pianists a body of music for expanding their left-hand technique, Godowsky was out to revolutionize piano composition itself. He prophesied: "If it is possible to assign to the left hand alone the work done usually by both hands simultaneously, what vistas are opened to future composers, were this attainment to be extended to both hands!" (Preface, p. 7).

Godowsky's prediction was wrong: his late-Romantic pyrotechnics, written at the end of a period in which the piano was king, proved to be a summit, an end rather than a beginning. But for later composers of left-hand music specifically, Godowsky's immense vocabulary of figurations and finger patterns must have been a great inspiration. It cannot be a coincidence that virtually all the well-written repertoire appeared *after* his Chopin *Studies*. For example, when Godowsky played in Moscow in 1905, Felix Blumenfeld (teacher of Vladimir Horowitz and Simon Barere) was so impressed by Godowsky's left-hand feats that he was moved to produce his own beautiful *Etude* the same year. The American composer John Corigliano claims that it was a performance by James Tocco of that Blumenfeld *Etude* which in turn inspired him to create his *Etude-Fantasy* for the American Bicentennial.

Interestingly, Godowsky said he began the great puzzle of transferring Chopin's thorny right-hand passagework to the left hand in an effort to take his mind off a terrible personal tragedy that occurred in 1893: he had just received the news that his in-laws had been killed in a railroad accident near Battle Creek, Michigan.[5] A compulsive worker, Godowsky could immerse himself in practice for fifteen hours a day and was only truly happy at the piano. Out of these initial efforts arose the 22 left-hand *Paraphrases on Chopin's Etudes*.

The discussion of Godowsky prompts the question: what does it mean to write well for the left hand alone? The standard piano literature for two hands partakes of our natural ability to play the bass and treble simultaneously; at times they are widely placed from one another. The bass line works *with* the melody, as in a Beethoven Symphony or a Verdi opera. In one-hand writing the major challenge is to work around the impossibility of being in two places at once. When the primary purpose of the composition is technical, it may be enough to move in single notes (with or without occasional doublings and added tones), as if writing for the violin or cello. This can be simple (see Ex.2) or very difficult (as in Ex.3).

EX. 2. **Saint-Saëns:** *Moto Perpetuo* **(Durand et fils, 1912), mm. 1–9.**

EX. 3. **Moszkowski:** *Etude* **no. 8 (Enoch & Cie., 1915), mm. 1–5.**

Problems arise in expressive, lyrical music, where the harmonic vocabulary is important and variety of texture essential. The best writers have found a way to achieve satisfying results by frequent lateral movements of the hand, made possible by delaying both bass and melody notes (see Exx.4 and 5). Godowsky was able to completely re-think the pianistic setting.

Scriabin too was ingenious (see Ex.6). Note the delay of the bass on the downbeats of measures 1, 2, 3, 4, and 8. But at the climax—the downbeat of measure 7—it is the melody which enters late. Variety is also achieved as the tied F (last note in measure 4) is effortlessly transformed from accompaniment to melody, now sounding in the middle of a three-voice texture.

The greatest pitfall for composers has been a kind of two-handed thinking, compelling the performer to insert many grace notes and broken chords (as in Exx.7 and

8). No amount of practice can make this sound right; unless a pianist is particularly enamored of the musical material, it is best avoided.

EX. 4. Chopin: *Etude*, op. 25, no. 5 (G. Schirmer, 1915), mm. 45–50.

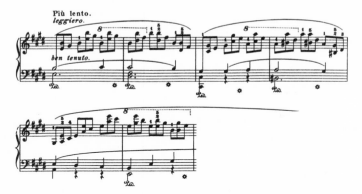

EX. 5. Chopin/Godowsky: *Etude*, op. 25, no. 5 (R. Lienau, 1899–1914), mm. 45–50.

EX. 6. Scriabin: *Nocturne* (Belaieff, 1895), mm. 1–8.

EX. 7. Zichy: *Sonata* (D. Rahter, 1887), mvt. 1, mm. 1–3.

EX. 8. Bach/Wittgenstein: *Sicilienne* (Universal, 1957), mm. 1–3.

It must have been the need to overcome obstacles, the heightened challenge to a composer's ingenuity that inspired the various fugues for left hand—see Kalkbrenner (he was the first), Reger, Bontoft, Takács, Dohnányi, and, above all, Godowsky—because the weaving of contrapuntal intricacies is precisely the task for which a single hand would seem the most *unlikely* candidate. But this sort of compositional challenge cannot be carried very far, for if composers were only interested in showing what they can accomplish with five fingers, without at the same time offering pianists the chance to "climb a mountain" (as Wittgenstein put it)—in other words if they *only* thought compositionally—would they not rather employ the highly developed right hand? And the hundreds of authors who created the repertoire have rarely chosen that hand. For most, the challenge of writing music within compositional limitations must be linked, in some sense, to the challenge of the performer mastering it with the *left* hand alone.

DISPLAY

Just as an etude for two hands may serve as a builder of technique as well as a demonstration of it, so with left-hand music. What could be more impressive than a solo display by that very hand which so often lags behind and now suddenly takes the spotlight? Consider also the very negative connotations stemming from its name—*gauche* in French, *sinistra* in Italian. For centuries this hand has been the one to avoid.

The immense number of salon pieces—sentimental tunes set in a modest technical framework—that were published on both sides of the Atlantic in the last part of the nineteenth century and well into the twentieth, indicates a thriving market of musical amateurs. We might call it "parlor music," for almost every middle-class parlor had a piano and a family member who could play it. It is easy to imagine an amateur pianist, especially before the age of recordings, when even concerts (particularly in America) were a relative rarity, making a fine impression with a rendition of even a modest left-hand number.

For master pianists the opportunities were more dramatic. For example, around the year 1900 two young pianists played debut recitals in Berlin, at that time the musical capital of the world. On these important occasions each chose left-hand music to grip the audience's attention. Béla Bartók's Berlin debut was his first significant concert

EX. 9. **The program for Bartók's Berlin debut, Dec. 14, 1903**

abroad. In his young years, before his absorption in folk music and the most forward-looking composition, Bartók was a virtuoso in the grand tradition: his big piece was the Liszt *Sonata* in B minor. The highlight of Bartók's Berlin program was his recently composed *Etude* for the left hand alone. Musically reminiscent of Strauss, this long and exciting movement calls for power, stamina, and first-class octaves in the manner of Liszt (see Ex.10).

Godowsky, who had returned to Berlin after ten years in the United States, welcomed the 22-year-old to his home, where Bartók was able to try out the left-hand *Etude* for Godowsky and his guests, among whom was the violinist Fritz Kreisler. Two days after his debut, Bartók wrote home to his teacher, István Thomán, the man to whom the *Study* was dedicated:

> The very significant Dec. 14th is over. . . . The Study for the left hand went splendidly; the greater part of the public was most impressed by this. The hall was quite two-thirds full. . . . Two "celebrities" were in the audience, Godowsky and Busoni. The latter came to the artist's room after the third part, introduced himself and congratulated me.[6]

EX. 10. Bartok: *Etude* (Kalmus, c. 1904?), mm. 1–5.

Bartók boasted to his mother as well: "I played a new work of my own with which I achieved much success. It is a sonata movement for the left hand only which sounds as if I played it with three hands. . . ."[7] While Bartók's image of "three hands" rather overstates the case, his success was a decisive one—Godowsky and Busoni were obviously impressed.

Leopold Godowsky was able to seal his Berlin triumph with the Chopin *Paraphrases*. His letter to Chicago critic W.S.B. Mathews (December 24, 1900), depicting the decisive turning point in a great career, bears witness to the kind of impact his *Paraphrases* could make on a cosmopolitan audience:

Imagine my surprise when I discovered that my concert was eagerly awaited by all musicians and music students. The Beethoven Hall was crowded with a representative musical audience. All Berlin pianists were at the concert. [After playing the Brahms *Concerto No. 1*] I came out to play my seven Chopin paraphrases. . . . The musicians and public did not know what to expect. There was a general commotion. The hall looked remarkably festive, and electricity was in the air. I played first the study for the left hand alone, op. 25, no. 4 (A minor) [Ex.11]. To describe the noise after this study would be impossible. The tremendous ovation was overwhelming. . . . To tell how many times I had to come out after the paraphrases would be impossible. I could not count them. Pianists like Pachmann, Josef Weiss, Hambourg, Anton Foerster and the entire audience actually went mad. They were screaming like wild beasts. I played as an encore the Black Key Study for the left hand [Ex.12]. I refused to play more. The scene in the artist's room will never be forgotten by those who have witnessed it. . . . All criticisms are so wonderful that I am told NOBODY ever got such notices. My success is the most sensational within the recollection of all musicians. Remember! I don't exaggerate the success—I can never do justice to it![8]

Godowsky was not exaggerating. As Arthur Abell later recalled:

Godowsky did things on the piano that evening that had never been heard before in this piano-ridden town. I shall never forget the unparalleled enthusiasm that his playing aroused. The next morning, all Berlin was ringing Godowsky's name; the newspapers came out with columns of eulogies, and the public was wild over him.[9]

EX. 11. Chopin/Godowsky: *Etude*, op. 25, no. 4 (R. Lienau, 1899–1914), mm. 1–2.

EX. 12. Chopin/Godowsky: *Etude*, op. 10, no. 5 (R. Lienau, 1899–1914), mm. 1–2.

The pioneers had come half a century earlier, when Alexander Dreyschock and Adolfo Fumagalli, two outstanding virtuosi of the 1840s and '50s, scored brilliant successes on the stages of Europe playing with their left hands alone. These trailblazers aroused an astonished reaction, almost amounting to disbelief, on the part of an adoring public and press. Only one work was definitely published before Dreyschock's entry into the left-hand arena, the modest study by Ludwig Berger already mentioned. And the *Etude* by the Parisian pianist Charles Thibault may also pre-date him. But we have no evidence that these works were publicly performed. Dreyschock's concert triumphs would stir others into action, and within a few years Alkan's mammoth *Fantaisie* appeared (c. 1846), as well as etudes by Czerny (1846) and Bovy-Lysberg (1848).

One thing is certain: Dreyschock and Fumagalli could never have advanced their careers an inch by performing solos for the *right* hand. For the glittery two-hand music created by these gentlemen, and indeed so much of the piano output of that entire school of early- and mid-nineteenth-century virtuosi, was already in a certain sense "for the right hand alone." In the writing of such influential composer/pianists as Johann Nepomuk Hummel (1778–1837), Sigismond Thalberg (1812–1871), and Henri Herz (1803–1888), the primary purpose was the display of digital skill involving the brilliant high registers of the piano, with the left hand playing only a supporting role.

The main purpose of a piano recital was to entertain and, if possible, to astonish. Novelty, display, and just plain *fun* were essential. There were sentimental character pieces and variations, pleasingly written in a virtuoso style; it was Herz* who pronounced,

---

*Herz, one of the first celebrated European artists to visit in the New World, really *should* have written for the left hand. From the last page of his memoir, *My Travels in America*, trans. Henry Hill (Madison: State Historical Society of Wisconsin, 1963), we learn: "From Mobile, Alabama I sailed to Jamaica, where cruel trials awaited me. Believing I had lost the use of my right hand, I endured crushing physical pain, accompanied by mental tortures a thousand times more disheartening. . . . Fortunately, the malady was not without cure, and three months after my arrival in Jamaica I was able to continue my concert tour through the two Americas."

"Parisians can understand and appreciate nothing but variations."[10] And above all there were opera paraphrases. This first great age of pianism coincided with a glorious regeneration of the Paris opera, and virtually all piano composers, great and small, leaned wisely on those beloved tunes originating at the opera house. As aptly expressed by Arthur Loesser: "It is safe to say that, to a considerable extent, the piano music of the years 1825–75 was a dependency of the opera."[11] Thus Fumagalli was able to crown his career with a left-hand *Fantasy* on Meyerbeer's uncannily popular *Robert le Diable.*

The sonatas of Mozart and Beethoven were fine for home consumption, but for public performers to offer the works of greater minds than their own (that is, to adhere to the twentieth-century conception of a piano recital) was a rare exception. Pianists played their own music, with repertoires tailored to their special skills. For example, Thalberg's stunt was to create the effect of three hands, with the two thumbs sharing the melody, as arpeggios swirled above and below; eventually he was nicknamed "Old Arpeggio." The high-minded Clara Wieck wrote despairingly to her future husband, Robert Schumann: "Won't you compose something brilliant and easy to understand for once? I want so much to have something of yours to play in public, something that suits the audience."[12] And Chopin lamented that the musical climate did not permit him to program Scarlatti!

In the early 1840s the solo piano recital was still in its infancy, and there was some fear that, despite the light-weight repertoire, the sound of a single instrument would prove monotonous. Variety was achieved by having a guest singer or instrumental group. Today we hesitate to applaud between the movements of a concerto, but our forebears thought nothing of bringing on an opera singer between movements to enliven the proceedings. Franz Liszt was the first to have the audacity to appear by himself for an entire evening on a regular basis, but in this irreverent atmosphere not even he was entirely safe. During one of his early recitals at La Scala, Milan, as he sat down to play a recent Study of his own devising, someone in the audience shouted: "I didn't come to the theater to *study*, I came to be entertained." Within several years, what Liszt called his "slavery to the public" drove him from the concert stage forever.

Crucial improvements had brought the piano to a new level of excellence, without which the great wave of virtuosi might not have been possible. The application of more metal to the predominantly wooden frame allowed for thicker and tighter strings, with a resulting increase in power and brilliance. Hammers were enlarged, and the covering changed from leather to the very superior felt. The full, singing tone stood in marked contrast to the sharp, thin sound of earlier days. Finally, a clever design by Sebastian Erard, called the double escapement, revolutionized the piano action, greatly facilitating repeated notes, trills, and all fast figurations—a generally improved responsiveness to the hand of a skilled player. And with the newly added, penetrating higher notes the modern piano was born.

The instrument was in its heyday, and the ever-growing middle class constituted not only a market for the sale of pianos but a vital audience for piano concerts. In the 1840s Paris seemed like the center of the world and performers flocked there in droves. Describing "pianomania" in an 1843 essay, Heinrich Heine, the great German poet and merciless critic, complained:

These pianos, which one can no longer avoid, which we hear sounding from every house, in all society day and night. . . . This eternal piano-playing is no longer to be endured. Ach! at this very moment my next-door neighbors, young daughters of Albion, are playing a brilliant morceau for two left hands. . . . This prevalence of piano-playing and the triumphal march of virtuosi are characteristic of our time and demonstrate the victory of machine over spirit. Technical skill, the precision of an automaton, the identification with strung wood, the mechanization of Man are now prized and celebrated as the highest Good. Like swarms of locusts the piano virtuosi come to Paris every winter, less to make money than to earn a name for themselves, which will yield all the more financial success for them in other countries. Paris serves as a kind of billboard where their fame may be read in gigantic letters. I say their fame is read there, because it is the Parisian press which proclaims it to the credulous world, and every virtuoso knows how to use both journals and journalists with the greatest virtuosity.[13]

The worship of Technique, the sheer number of pianists vying for attention, the importance of reviews, and a Parisian success—all this played a part. The jibe at left-hand playing was certainly directed at Alexander Dreyschock, the most recent and promising star on the pianistic horizon. In a remarkably successful effort to stand out above that "swarm of locusts," Dreyschock had hit upon the ultimate stunt.

2.

Alexander Dreyschock

1818–1869

The first pianist known to perform in public with his left hand alone was a likely candidate for the honor: the Czech-born Alexander Dreyschock had a lifelong fascination with his left hand. Through fanatical practice—and he was a great worker—he developed it to the point where the "dean" of pianists, Johann Baptist Cramer, once said to him, "You don't have a left hand; you have two right hands!" Thirds, sixths, and octaves were Dreyschock's specialties.

William Mason, who took one hundred piano lessons from Dreyschock in Prague, told an interesting story in his *Memories of Musical Life*.[1] One day Vaclav Tomasek, Dreyschock's teacher, was discussing recent dramatic strides in piano technique. Pointing to the score of Chopin's *"Revolutionary" Etude*, he prophesied that some day a pianist would play the left-hand part in octaves instead of single notes. As it stands, Chopin's study is a difficult finger-twister for the left hand; to perform it *allegro* in octaves would be something like running a mile in 3½ minutes. But Dreyschock took the dare, went home, and glued himself to his piano bench. After practicing twelve hours a day for six weeks he emerged victorious. We will never know the actual tempo at which he managed his *"Revolutionary"* in octaves, but it was good enough to astonish Mendelssohn when Dreyschock played it at the Leipzig Gewandhaus concerts.

It is not possible to pinpoint exactly when Dreyschock took the plunge, but his natural facility, together with his obsession for left-hand difficulties were natural stepping stones to music for the left hand alone. Actually, in the years preceding Dreyschock's career, a few left-hand pieces had appeared in print, but there is no evidence that any of them were performed in public. The audiences at his concerts appeared to be experiencing something utterly novel, and the critics mentioned no precedents. Whether Dreyschock was driven by a need for notoriety or was simply responding to a great inner challenge—or both—it was the smartest thing he ever did.

After four years of study with Tomasek, Dreyschock stormed out of Prague. In 1839, when he was 21, the *Revue et gazette musicale* anticipated his approach to Paris as if heralding the advance of enemy troops:

> A German [he was Czech!] pianist, Alexander Dreyschock, is presently traveling in Prussia and Hanover; everywhere he causes a furor. We are assured that as far as mechanism and prodigious digital facility are concerned, he is the most astonishing player, and that when he arrives in Paris he will prove a dangerous rival for Liszt, Thalberg and Döhler.[2]

Things moved much more slowly in those days, and it was four more seasons before Dreyschock actually got to Paris. When he finally burst on the scene, the prestigious *Revue* portrayed a new pianistic trinity, with Liszt as the Father, Thalberg the Son, and Dreyschock the Holy Ghost—no mean achievement for a 24-year-old from Zak.

In 1843, at his first Paris concerts, Dreyschock played his own solo compositions, as was the custom. But he appeared alone, without the assistance of a singer or other artists. This practice was still new enough to merit special notice, and, to one critic's surprise, the listeners' faces registered no signs of boredom throughout the evening. Among Dreyschock's offerings was a work for the left hand alone. Critic Henri Blanchard loved the concerts but kept his distance from these "variations for the left hand alone, a kind of *tour de force* more curious to see than it is gracious to hear; the inextricable difficulties are its principal merit . . . but what are these *lapsus manus* in the incessant jumps of a single hand which does the work of two?"[3]

Dreyschock's compositions were as short on musical meaning as they were long on technical difficulties, and, like other composer-pianists of the day, he suited the writing to his particular digital skills. What was his playing like? Reading old music reviews is fun, not least for the authentic atmosphere and revelation of cultural attitudes. However, in the nineteenth century both audiences and critics were nearly always hearing the music for the first time, thus the response could be fresh and enthusiastic, but also uncritical. Written impressions must be taken with a large grain of salt, and in Dreyschock's case the impressions are contradictory. The witty Heine wrote:

> I can truly report that public opinion has declared him one of the greatest of pianists and compared him with the most celebrated. He makes a hellish noise [höllischen Spektakel]. One believes he is hearing not the pianist Dreyschock but rather three times sixty [drei Schock] pianists . . . it is easy to burst an eardrum when this piano-beater lets loose. Hang yourself, Franz Liszt, you are a common wind idol [Windgötze] in comparison with this God of Thunder.[4]

Hector Berlioz had only praise for this "young man, whose talent is fresh, brilliant and energetic, with immense technical skill and musical feeling of the highest order."[5]

The young Hans von Bülow, finding himself up against Dreyschock in Vienna and unable to present a recital before the Czech phenomenon had left town, wrote home to his parents that his adversary was "an homme machine, the personification of absence of genius, with the exterior of a clown."[6]

Though Bülow was put down, Dreyschock could never de-throne "Liszt the Father."

A short time after Dreyschock had shaken up the Viennese public with his "*Revolutionary*" Etude in left-hand octaves, Liszt decided to show who was boss. At *his* next Viennese concert, after rippling through Chopin's Etude in F minor, op. 25, no. 2, Liszt played the opening notes in octaves, slowly and hesitantly. Then he accelerated into a lightning-fast performance of the entire piece—in octaves. The two artists must have reconciled, for in later years Dreyschock visited Liszt at Weimar.

Piano music tells us something about the playing of its creator. Just as, for example, the first version of Liszt's Paganini *Etudes* reveals Liszt's phenomenal powers (Schumann said only six pianists in Europe would be able to master them), so does the writing by Dreyschock for the left hand alone tell us much about him. If he could play the arrangement shown in Ex.13 at anything like the required tempo, he had a very good left hand indeed.

EX. 13. **Dreyschock:** *Variations on God Save the Queen* (André, 1862), mm. 17–19.

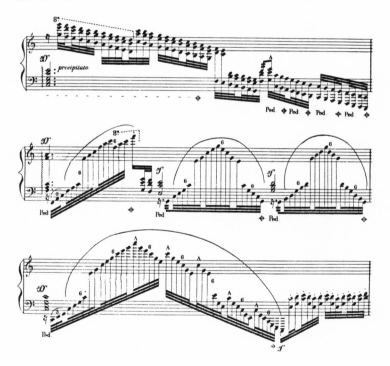

Dreyschock went to London, where the *Times* credited him with "an execution equal to that of Thalberg and Liszt"[7] (will critics never tire of pitting one famous performer against another?) and reported that his left-hand music was "most enthusiastically applauded."[8] While there, Dreyschock met Ignaz Moscheles, who corroborated the reports about Dreyschock's technical facility but dismissed his talents as a musician:

He is still young in the art, but his powers as an executant are marvelous; he has an exquisite delicate touch and performs astonishing "tours de force" with his left hand; but alas! His playing is restricted to twelve pieces, which he has toiled at incessantly. He has no style and cannot read music."[9]

How can we reconcile that "exquisite delicacy of touch" with Heine's depiction of a deafening "piano-beater"? And if Dreyschock was the musical ignoramus Moscheles depicts, why would Anton Rubinstein invite him to teach at the newly founded St. Petersburg Conservatory, as he did in 1862?

In that single London season Dreyschock gave a total of fifteen concerts, and the next dozen years took him to Belgium, Holland, Germany, Austria, Hungary, Denmark, and Sweden. In Brussels the audience loudly demanded a repetition of his left-hand *Variations*. The same work caused a sensation in Copenhagen, and when he left the King of Denmark gave him a box of cigars wrapped in 100-thaler bank notes.

Not only Heine poked fun at Dreyschock. As his fame grew, poems appeared in his honor, including one by the Viennese critic Moritz Gottlieb Saphir:

> Welchen Titel der nicht hinke
> Man dem Meister geben möchte,
> Der zur Rechten macht die Linke?—
> Nennt ihn, "Doctor beider Rechte."[10]

(What title which doesn't "limp" can we give to the Master who makes a right hand out of his left hand? Call him "Doctor of Both Right Hands.")

Two tributes took a musical form. Eduard Marxsen, later the teacher of Brahms, gave his *Three Left Hand Impromptus* the subtitle "*Hommage à Dreyschock*"; and Leschetizky's arrangement of the Sextet from *Lucia di Lammermoor* was dedicated to Dreyschock.

The invitation to teach in St. Petersburg was an honor, but it proved fatal—the Russian climate was too much for Dreyschock. He traveled to Italy for his health, only to die in Venice at the age of 51. Of the many piano works Dreyschock produced and performed, only two were for the left hand alone. But they were dazzling and they were all he needed: his listeners had never heard anything like them.

3.

Adolfo Fumagalli

1828–1856

The next pianist to make his mark on the public playing left-handed was a young Italian from Inzago. Ten years younger than Dreyschock, Adolfo Fumagalli came from a remarkable family: all four brothers were professional pianists and published composers. (The youngest, Luca, toured America successfully and settled in Philadelphia.) Adolfo was probably the best and certainly the most successful. He studied at the Milan Conservatory as a star pupil of Angeleri and made his debut in that city.

When Fumagalli came to Paris in 1849, critic Henri Blanchard was only partly impressed, finding him "a Milanese pianist with a young, feminine physique and fingers of iron or steel; he plays the piano strongly and well; but he paraphrases a little too much. . . ."[1] How many opera medleys did poor Blanchard have to sit through in the six years since our last encounter with him from Dreyschock's day? The irony here is that Fumagalli's opera paraphrases are easily his best music; his many original compositions offer virtually nothing behind their showy exteriors. With an opera transcription we are at least guaranteed the worthy tunes of Verdi or Bellini. (Fumagalli's music is almost impossible to locate in the United States, though there are several pieces for piano *two* hands in Volume XVI of *L'arte antiche e moderne: scelta di compositioni per pianoforte* [Milan: Ricordi, c. 1863].)

Fumagalli appeared regularly in the French capital, and within three years Blanchard was crediting him as "the first serious pianist who has come to us from Italy."[2] Here the critic is conveniently forgetting Muzio Clementi, the founder of modern pianism! Fumagalli's concerts were more or less successful, but only in 1855, when he brought in his heavy artillery, did he score a sensation. In January of that year, at the

Salle Herz, he performed his *Fantasy* on Meyerbeer's opera *Robert le Diable*, a 27-page blockbuster for the left hand alone. It brought down the house:

> A grand bravura fantasy on motives from *Robert le Diable* composed and executed in an overwhelming manner by the composer, so that if one were told to close one's eyes during the performance of this exceptional étude and also told that it was being played by two or even four hands, one would absolutely believe it; and one would only be disabused of this auditory illusion upon opening one's eyes and seeing the gloved right hand of the pianist resting quietly on his thigh while the left performs this astounding prestidigitation. Piano music and piano virtuosi have their dilettanti as Italian singing does: the *tour de force* was greeted with bravos and the composer called back three times.[3]

Blanchard may have been tired of opera fantasies, but he obviously had not been astonished by anyone's left hand since Dreyschock.

According to Fumagalli's biographer Filippo Filippi, another Paris critic was momentarily fooled by what he heard that evening:

> The first time he played it [the *Robert Fantasy*] at the Salle Herz, the public stood up to see if it really was one hand playing with such strength and sending such a cloud of notes into the air. Scudo, France's greatest critic, was fooled himself. Having arrived at the concert a little late, just as Adolfo was playing the *Robert Fantasy*, he stood in the back, behind the crowd, listening and without looking at his program. He thought he was hearing the usual piece for two hands and gave warm signs of approval, when he heard one of his neighbors say "It's impossible that this is one hand." At these words Scudo looked closely at his program, stretched his neck and saw the artist's gloved hand resting on his knee. Scudo, usually so reserved and sparing of praise could not resist shouting "Bravo!" and declaring his admiration afterwards in the pages of the *Revue des deux Mondes*.[4]

This story does not quite ring true in certain details—we have heard about that gloved hand before. And a careful search of the *Revue* did not uncover a review by Scudo. In fact, Filippi's *Della vita e delle opere di Adolfo Fumagalli* is a strange little book, quite devoid of biographical facts and filled with absurd claims placing Fumagalli comfortably alongside Chopin and Liszt. It provides very little information about the actual man, but the reader comes away with the vague feeling that if Fumagalli had lived a normal life span he might have surpassed the three B's. This book exemplifies the difficulty of obtaining substantive material on minor nineteenth-century musical figures. Filippi's biography is the only source of information about the career of this colorful artist. A multitude of short encyclopedia articles about Fumagalli—in all languages—which appeared in subsequent decades dutifully reproduce the same handful of tidbits from this book. For example, Filippi claimed that Fumagalli was dubbed "the Paganini of the Piano,"[5] so every writer repeated this title, but Filippi does not say who called him a Paganini. It is not impossible that he simply made it up.

Another listener at Fumagalli's big concert was A.P. Fiorentino. Like Blanchard, he was impressed, but he ended his comments ironically. He described Fumagalli as "a pianist whose force and talent are truly extraordinary. . . . What astonished the listener most was the *Fantasy* on *Robert le Diable*, which he plays with the left hand alone, persuading us that God gave us a right hand so that we would not use it."[6]

The left hand is kept busy (see Ex.14), but the form is primitive. A study of the paraphrase on music from the same opera by Liszt—which he played with electrifying effect in the same city—reveals telling differences of thematic and structural ingenuity. But these aesthetic questions faded in importance, since Fumagalli was able to score such a sensational pianistic point. It was with poetic justice that he dedicated his left-hand *Robert Fantasy* to Franz Liszt.

EX. 14. **Fumagalli:** *Fantasy on Robert le Diable* (**G. Ricordi, c. 1850**), **mm. 105–122.**

Later that year the pianist presented his left-hand version of the great aria "Casta Diva" from Bellini's *Norma*. Blanchard gushed: "Monsieur Fumagalli 'sang' it with one hand as if, laughing at the greatest difficulties, he were playing with two."[7] The novelty of the medium and the music worked to the pianist's benefit, for this transcription is quite devoid of "the greatest difficulties." (Actually, it is rather easy; see below, Ex.27, p.55.)

Fumagalli's prestige grew, and on his return to perform in his native Italy, the Erard firm sent along one of its concert grands for his personal use. Like Dreyschock, Fumagalli was heard at the royal court in Denmark. In Brussels, as always, the left-hand *Robert Fantasy* made his name:

> It is there that M. Fumagalli was truly prodigious. In general we are not very partial to *tours de force* in music, but this one deserves all the applause lavished on it by the public. With one hand the artist occupies the entire keyboard, simultaneously he plays the melody in the middle, an accompaniment in the bass and embroidery in the upper octaves. These three parts proceed together, in a sustained manner, with perfect clarity and a great variety of effects. One doubts the possibility of what one is hearing.[8]

This Belgian critic went all the way and compared him favorably with Liszt, noting that Fumagalli was quieter when seated at the piano, "without those tender looks, distortions of the face, the pantomime of being beside himself. . . ."[9] (This slap at Liszt is a reminder that calm repose always had its strong adherents. The fans of Josef Wölfl preferred him to Beethoven because of his great calm. Liszt did express intense inner feeling by making faces, and, on at least one occasion, he fainted while playing in public.)

With wonderful reviews, a mountain of effective salon pieces, and that crucial half-dozen left-hand opera paraphrases in his fingers, Fumagalli seemed on the verge of a great European career. But on a brief stop in Florence, he contracted cholera and died at the age of 28. Italy lost its most celebrated pianist.

Perhaps, in one sense, it was just as well. The times were changing: by the year 1860—and Fumagalli would have been only 32 years old—the whole idea of the composer/pianist as a purveyor of his own feather-weight concoctions was fading. Thalberg had retired to Italy to grow grapes, and Herz was teaching. A new generation of pianists—Hans von Bülow, Anton Rubinstein, the mature Clara Schumann—would dedicate the greater part of their careers to presenting the music of others. They were vessels, bringing to life the creations of Beethoven, Schumann, Chopin, and others greater than themselves. Perhaps Fumagalli would have been like the silent film stars who, when the talkies came in, found themselves without a voice.

EX. 15 (opposite). Poster for Adolfo Fumagalli's benefit concert at the Milan Conservatory. No. 3 is his left-hand arrangement of Bellini's "Casta Diva"; in No. 6 his brothers Luca and Polibio took part in a work for eight pianists, while Disma appears as a composer in No. 8. The program—an alternation of solo and ensemble piano music with operatic repertoire—is typical of the format with which pianists presented themselves to the public in the mid-nineteenth century.

I. R. CONSERVATORIO DI MUSICA

Per la sera di Venerdì 28 Dicembre 1855 alle ore 8 precise

QUINTO CONCERTO DI A. FUMAGALLI

A BENEFICIO DEL PIO RICOVERO PEI BAMBINI LATTANTI

coadjuvato da alcuni Allievi di Canto d'ambo i sessi dell'I. R. Conservatorio suddetto.

PROGRAMMA

PARTE I.ª

1.ª SINFONIA nell'Opera il *Flauto Magico*, per quattro pianoforti, eseguita dai signori **Carlo Rovere**, **Luigi Erba**, **Vibulano Dall'Acqua** e **Luigi Rivetta** . . . . **MOZART**

2.ª DUETTO per due Soprani nell'Opera *Celini a Parigi*, eseguito dalle allieve **Iturbida Narial ed Elisa Galli** (con accompagnamento di pianoforte) . . . **LAURO ROSSI**

3.ª (a) *Casta Diva*, nella *Norma*. — ANDANTE-STUDIO per la sola mano sinistra.
(b) *La Buena Ventura*. — CANZONE ANDALUSA, composta ed eseguita da . . . **A. FUMAGALLI**

4.ª DUETTO per Soprano e Tenore nell'Opera *Lucrezia Borgia*, eseguito dall'allievo **Giuseppe Limberti** e dall'allieva **Iturbida Narial** . . . . **DONIZETTI**

5.ª *Io Sacrilega* parola. Finale nell'Opera il *Poliuto*, trascritto e variato da . . . **A. FUMAGALLI**

PARTE II.ª

6.ª SINFONIA dell'Opera *Semiramide*, per quattro pianoforti a quattro mani, eseguita dai signori **Carlo Rovere**, **Carlo Andreoli**, **Luigi Erba**, **Potibio Fumagalli**, **Vibulano Dall'Acqua**, **Luca Fumagalli**, **Giovanni Morganti**, e **Luigi Rivetta** . . . **ROSSINI**

7.ª CAVATINA nell'Opera *Lucia di Lammermoor*, eseguita dall'allieva **Elisa Galli** . . . . **DONIZETTI**

8.ª (a) *Courage, pauvre mère!* MELODIA di F. *Bonoldi*, variata ed eseguita da **A. FUMAGALLI**
(b) *Bella Figlia dell'amore*. QUARTETTO nell'Opera *Rigoletto*, eseguito da **Adolfo Fumagalli**, e composto da suo fratello . . . **DISMA FUMAGALLI**

9.ª ROMANZA nell'Opera *Luisa Miller*, eseguita dall'allievo **Gius. Limberti** . . . **VERDI**

10.ª SCENA ed ARIA per Soprano nell'Opera *La Traviata*, eseguita dall'allieva **Iturbida Narial** . . . . **VERDI**

11.ª (a) *Preghiera alla Madonna*. MELODIA popolare di **Gordigiani**, variata
(b) *Il Carnovale di Venezia*, composto ed eseguito da . . . **A. FUMAGALLI**

Biglietto d'ingresso "L. 3. — Per una sedia fissa in Sala oppure sul Palco Scenico "L. 3.

I Biglietti trovansi vendibili presso i signori Editori di musica RICORDI, LUCA *e* CANTI, *ed alla sera stessa alla porta dell' I. R. Conservatorio.*

Un apposito Bacile riceverà le offerte spontanee.

La Sala sarà aperta alle ore sette.

4.

Geza Zichy

1849–1924

In May 1915, a remarkable concert took place in Berlin: a one-armed pianist gave a recital for one-armed men. The pianist was Count Geza Zichy, and the audience consisted solely of men crippled during the first year of World War I. The purpose of the concert, and the following lecture, was inspirational: Zichy wanted to lift these soldiers from their despair, to prove to them that they too could be whole men again.

Zichy's early life read like a fairy tale. Born into an old and distinguished Hungarian family, Count Geza grew up in a setting of fabulous wealth and the highest social privilege. He began to play the piano at age five and showed some talent, although his first teacher judged that his left hand would never accomplish anything! On a hunting expedition when he was fifteen, he tried to pull his rifle from the back of a cart just as one of the horses lurched. The gun went off, shattering his right arm. It was amputated at the shoulder.

After the excruciating physical pain of the first days had subsided, the even greater psychological anguish set in. With superhuman pluck, Zichy pulled himself together. He gave his private tutor a sealed letter, with instructions to open it a year later. It said: "If exactly one year from today I am unable to do with one hand what other people can do with two, put a bullet through my head."[1] Zichy's servant pitied him, but

> I chased him out of the room, locked the door and dressed myself. It took three hours, but I did it. I used the door knob, the furniture, my feet and my teeth to achieve it. At meals I ate no food which I could not cut myself, and today I peel apples, clip my fingernails, ride, drive a four in hand, I am a good shot and have even learned to play the piano a little.[2]

Zichy's deepest sufferings lay ahead: "With real anguish I avoided going near my piano. Those white keys seemed to grin at me like the teeth of a skeleton's skull."[3] Zichy finally tried a little playing with one hand, but slammed the cover down in despair. Then after some time had passed,

> I got a piano teacher—a hard, merciless woman . . . my arm got stronger, my fingers turned to steel. I wanted to play the piano and began to use my thumb as a right hand. I was an empiricist. I didn't ponder over theories of one-hand piano playing; I knew nothing about how it could be done, but I did it.[4]

The remarkable thing about Zichy is that he seems to have determined upon a career as a pianist only *after* losing his right arm. Another story reveals his spunk. Of course, hunting was the cause of his tragedy and was now forbidden.

> I sneaked out of the castle with my weapon on my back. My father caught me. He frowned and asked in a stern voice "Who gave you permission to go hunting?" "I myself, dear father. I want to and I will be a whole man." The old soldier took me in his arms and stammered through tears, "Right, my son, my dear son."[5]

Zichy's autobiography, *Aus meinem Leben*, is very sketchy about his subsequent musical development. The turning point came in 1875—Zichy was 26 years old—when both his arrangement and his performance of Schubert's song "Der Erlkönig" impressed Franz Liszt. He encouraged the young man to publish six *Etudes* ("Der Erlkönig" was one of them), and contributed a flattering preface himself. Around 1880, Zichy began his concert career in earnest, with about fifteen left-hand pieces of his own devising. Only a few were published, and they are hard to locate today. His concerts generated great interest. Europe had seen Dreyschock and Fumagalli with their virtuoso forays into one-hand playing. But they had two hands and used both of them nearly all the time. This was something completely different—a man who had to generate an entire concert using the only hand he had. As Liszt reported to his friend Olga von Meyendorff, "Geza Zichy created a sensation at a recent concert (the first time that he has favored Budapest with his extraordinary virtuosity). The hall was packed and his success complete" (Budapest, January 31, 1879).[6]

Zichy made no recordings, and his career is only sketchily documented. We have the enthusiastic report of Eduard Hanslick, writing of Zichy's second visit to Vienna in 1882. The usually reserved Hanslick waxed enthusiastic:

> The most astounding thing we have heard in the way of piano playing in recent times has been accomplished by a one-armed man—Count Geza Zichy. Many can play, some can enchant, but Zichy is the only one who can work miracles. . . . Count Zichy displayed a marvelous and astonishing volume of tone in a "Concert Etude" and a Hungarian fantasy, both of his own composition, and then in Bach's Chaconne, arranged by himself for the left hand, and his lightning-like jumps, skips and glides and his polyphonic legato playing were so extraordinary that his listeners could scarcely believe their ears and eyes."[7]

Liszt, always candid in writing to his confidante the Baroness von Meyendorff, confirmed the impression: "Geza Zichy's reputation is not just parochial Hungarian. He is an astonishing artist of the left hand, which is remarkably dexterous to the point that the greatest pianists would be hard put to match him" (Budapest, February 18, 1882).[8]

Not only was Zichy the first one-armed pianist in history, but his career was remarkable in another sense. Because of his great wealth and social standing, he felt it was wrong to take a fee for his performances. Every penny he earned was given to charity. According to the Paris press, by 1886 he had raised and given away well over a million francs. He claimed that the returns from a single concert in Trieste saved the homes of an entire street of poor people who were about to be evicted.

Zichy's concerts were not merely musical events, but social occasions of the first magnitude. His aristocratic connections were such that for his German debut, given in Munich, thirteen royal princes sat in the first row. In fact, with the exception of King Ludwig II, who never attended large gatherings, almost every dignitary and ambassador in the city was in the audience. Zichy could have performed for the eccentric monarch in private (Wagner had arranged private musicales for Ludwig) but it would have meant playing behind a screen. Zichy refused.

His tours took him from his native Hungary to Italy, Scandinavia, and Russia. When he played for the king and queen of Denmark, the Princess of Wales—the future queen of England—was in attendance. The guests of honor were Czar Alexander III of Russia and the czarina. While Zichy played, the czar kept shouting out compliments, and between musical selections he came over to the pianist and carefully examined each of his five fingers. At the lavish banquet following the concert, the guests—as always happened—wanted to help him eat. Zichy silenced them by peeling an apple for each of the ladies at the table.

Where aristocratic connections did not suffice, Zichy had his devoted mentor, Franz Liszt, to pave the way with letters of introduction to colleagues. When Zichy came onstage to give his first Paris concert, Gounod, Saint-Saëns, Massenet, and Delibes were sitting in the first row. Liszt also performed with Zichy on Hungarian stages several times, in the latter's three-hand arrangement of the *Rácóczy March*. Two of these performances took place in Hungarian towns where Liszt had not appeared since his young years, and the furor in the audience was indescribable. He also played at least once with the violinist Joseph Joachim—most likely performing Zichy's *Hungarian Fantasy* (which was probably never published).

Zichy's two-volume memoir, *Aus meinem Leben,* is the main source of information about this remarkable pianist. But it has many gaps, and one wishes that certain subjects had been treated more fully. In the 1880s Zichy published about fifteen original pieces, in addition to some transcriptions from Bach, Chopin, and Wagner. But exactly which works did he play at his concerts? Did he take an interest in—and perform—left-hand music by other composers? (Rudolph Niemann's *Drei Klavierstücke,* op. 40, are dedicated to Zichy, as is the superb *Etude* of Emil Sauer.) Why did Zichy publish no piano music during the last forty years of his life? He created the first concerto for left hand and orchestra but mentions no performances.

Though many questions were left unanswered, Zichy partly atoned for that with a vivid portrait of his idol Liszt, the man he called "the most beautiful memory of my life." This is the calm, melancholy Liszt of the last years, who sat at his piano quietly improvising unheard-of harmonies. The old master's heart must have gone out to this young man whose fate was so painful and unusual. And he surely approved of Zichy's sense of *noblesse oblige*—the charity concerts seem modeled on his own career. Liszt encouraged Zichy's efforts as a composer and sent his *Etudes* around to friends and students. In the very last weeks of his life Liszt was writing to Zichy about the latter's left-hand *Sonata*, praising it far beyond its worth and plotting to get it published. (However, as Zichy himself noted, what musician, however obscure, did *not* receive a generous response from this saint of music, especially in his later years?)

Liszt produced for Zichy's use an arrangement of one of his own last songs, "Hungary's God," the only left-hand work he ever composed. He rejoiced in Zichy's first successes and gave Zichy advice on transcribing the Bach *Chaconne* for violin. (Here we learn that Liszt himself had worked out many variations on the same *Chaconne*.) It was not all one-way: Zichy's home and well-spread table were always at the disposal of Liszt, who stayed with the Zichy family for weeks at a time in a small house built expressly for him. And Zichy supplied his teacher with the best cognac, a drink Liszt seems to have consumed in large quantities.

They often traveled together, and it was Zichy who accompanied Liszt on an emotional return to the village Raiding, his birthplace. When Liszt left the town as an eleven-year-old prodigy, the peasant women had prophesied that the pianist would some day return in a glass coach, so celebrated would he be. So Zichy had the inspired idea of outfitting a beautiful glass coach, and they entered the town in triumph.

In the last decades of his life Zichy branched out and became a powerful figure in Hungary's musical life, serving for 43 years as the director of the National Conservatory. His appointment as intendant of the Royal Opera caused the resignation of Gustav Mahler, who knew that Zichy stood against his Germanization of the repertoire there. Zichy wrote five operas to his own texts, and some of the poems in *Aus meinem Leben* reveal a distinct literary talent.

Zichy's training as a composer was under Robert Volkmann. Considering his limitations in composition it seems rather strange that Zichy did not use his wealth to enrich his repertoire with commissions from great colleagues, as Paul Wittgenstein would later do. Incidentally, these two one-armed pianists knew each other slightly and the older man may have inspired the younger. Bartók was moved to write his left-hand *Etude* after hearing a concert by his fellow-countryman, and many other listeners were probably strongly affected by the unique sight of this man coming onstage.

One of Zichy's finest accomplishments had no connection with the piano: *Das Buch des Einarmigen* (The Book of the One-Armed), in which Zichy gave advice on acquiring the skills to live independently. With exercises, explanations, and 40 photographs, the handicapped reader learned to use his one hand—and two feet—in ways he would not have devised himself. The number of crippled soldiers in World War I was tragically high, and the book must have had many readers, for it went through five printings.

5.

Paul Wittgenstein

1887–1961

Of the many soldiers for whom Zichy wrote his book, the thousands whose bodies and lives were shattered by World War I, one man was destined for a musical career far greater than Zichy himself had achieved.

At first the young Austrian pianist Paul Wittgenstein seemed to have everything. His family stood at the pinnacle of Viennese society. Paul's father had made a great fortune in America, returning to Austria as the "Iron King." The Wittgenstein salon was a stopping point for the cultural elite in turn-of-the-century Vienna. As a child Paul sat at elegant dinner parties alongside Brahms and Clara Schumann; it was in his living room that the clarinet sonatas of Brahms were first performed. Casals was there with Bruno Walter, and Mahler too. On the walls hung the paintings of Klimt, and on the pianos lay priceless manuscripts of Bach and Mozart. According to Brahms, the family treated one another as if they were at court.

The Wittgenstein passion for excellence was palpable, the children furiously driven to excel. Two of Paul's brothers cracked under the strain and committed suicide, but another, Ludwig, became a distinguished philosopher. Paul showed musical promise and, after initial studies with Leschetizky, made his debut in Vienna at age 26. The next season he was a concerto soloist with the Vienna Symphony.

Called up for service at the front, Wittgenstein was gravely wounded near the Polish border, and his right arm had to be amputated. As a prisoner of the Russians he spent some months in a Siberian camp, where he managed to find a piano to practice on. As soon as the Russians released him he was back in the German army fighting at the Italian front.

While Zichy had been an amateur pianist of fifteen when he lost his arm, Wittgenstein was already an aspiring professional musician. Permanently back home in Vienna, he refused to give up his piano. Leschetizky had died, but Wittgenstein worked alone for seven hours a day, keeping his teacher's principles before him, particularly the idea of a loose wrist. "It was like climbing a mountain" he later said, "if you can't get up one way, you try another."[1] Wittgenstein was determined to be a pianist in spite of all, but what music would he play? For several years he looked for repertoire in libraries. Although as a performer Zichy was an inspiring predecessor—the two had a passing acquaintance—Wittgenstein found Zichy's music trivial. Wittgenstein admired the Brahms transcription of Bach's *Chaconne*, the *Etudes* of Saint-Saëns and Reger, and the lyrical *Prelude and Nocturne* by Scriabin. From hundreds of German salon pieces he correctly singled out the superior compositions of Alexis Hollaender, and he was taken with Godowsky's diabolically clever *Chopin Paraphrases*. To this rather small group he added his own transcriptions from opera, lieder, and the two-hand piano literature.

Wittgenstein had no pretensions as an original composer, but instead had the inspired idea of using his considerable wealth for a series of commissions. In 1916 he made his return to the stage with a *Konzertstück* by his composition teacher, Joseph Labor. The list of colleagues from whom he soon commissioned works reads like a *Who's Who* of 1920s Vienna: Schütt, Braun, Gal, Bricht, Korngold, Schmidt, and Strauss. Wittgenstein must have realized that a one-armed pianist has a greater chance of success in a concerto or a chamber work than in a solo composition. With orchestral instruments filling out the texture and harmony—as they do in a violin concerto—there is no need for great ingenuity on the composer's part; the number of hands becomes, to a certain extent, a moot point. And the première of a concerto by a major composer is a stellar event: at the height of his career, particularly after receiving the Ravel *Concerto* and the Britten *Diversions*, Wittgenstein was a soloist with the world's great orchestras, playing under such conductors as Walter, Mengelberg, Monteux, Furtwängler, Kleiber, Koussevitzky, and Ormandy.

All together, Wittgenstein was the recipient of about forty works. "Since it is no particular attainment of mine I think I may honestly say that I am (perhaps) the pianist for whom the greatest number of special compositions have been written."[2] The fees he paid to his composers must have been considerable: Hindemith was able to furnish his entire house in Frankfurt, and Franz Schmidt was finally able to buy the home he had long wanted. Most of the composers put up with strenuous complaints, for Wittgenstein had a pugnacious spirit and relished a good battle with his colleagues. The Strauss *Parergon* was not half brilliant enough for him, and he made the composer write a second work. Wittgenstein was also very conservative in his musical tastes and made no secret of it. One can feel Hindemith cringing as he writes to the pianist, "I would be really sorry if the piece didn't please. Perhaps, at first, it will sound a bit unusual to you. I've written it with great affection and like it very much."[3] The work did not "please" at all: Wittgenstein never played it, the manuscript is lost, and the Hindemith *Concerto* has completely disappeared.

Prokofieff too was nervous about the way *Concerto* No. 4 might be received. He already knew of Wittgenstein's dissatisfaction with Strauss's work and the changes Wittgenstein had made in Ravel's *Concerto*. Prokofieff wrote to the pianist:

I hope from both the pianistic viewpoint as well as from one considering the orchestra and piano combined, that this concerto will give you satisfaction. I have racked my brains trying to predict what sort of impression it will make upon you as music. Difficult problem! You are a musician of the 19th century, I am of the 20th. I have tried to compose as simply as possible; for your part, don't judge the piano part too hastily, if certain moments seem to be indigestible at first, don't press yourself to pronounce judgement, but wait a while. If you contemplate any improvements which we could make in this concerto, don't hesitate to share them with me.[4]

As with Hindemith, so with Prokofieff. He soon received a letter stating "I thank you for the Concerto, but I don't understand one note of it and I won't play it!"

Wittgenstein evidently liked a lot of sound and did not hesitate to change the solo parts to suit himself. According to British conductor Trevor Harvey, who worked with Wittgenstein, this tampering annoyed composer Benjamin Britten when it came time to perform his *Diversions*.[5]

At the first meeting between Ravel and Wittgenstein, the pianist was disappointed in the work that had been created for him. (Ravel, no great shakes as a pianist, had to use two hands to play it.) A later meeting caused the greatest scandal of Wittgenstein's career. Marguerite Long, who had been traveling with Ravel, told the story:

We heard the Concerto in Vienna, during the course of a European concert tour, at the home of the dedicatee, Paul Wittgenstein. He had received it a few months before and had already played it in public in the Austrian capital on Nov. 27th, 1931. We were invited to a grand dinner at his house, followed by a soirée. The Quartet was played and the master of the house was to play the Concerto with the accompaniment of a second piano, so that Ravel could finally hear his work. I was a little nervous, because during dinner, I was seated to the right of Wittgenstein, who confided in me that he had been obliged to make certain "arrangements" in the work. In my heart I excused him because I believed his physical handicap responsible for these liberties; I advised him to tell Ravel in advance. He did not do so. During the performance, I was following with the score of the Concerto, which I still did not know and was able to observe on Ravel's ever-darkening face the misdeeds of our host's initiatives. As soon as it was finished, I and the ambassador Clauzel attempted a diversion to avoid an incident. Alas! Ravel slowly advanced toward Wittgenstein and said to him, "But that is not it at all." And the other defended himself, "I am an old pianist and that doesn't sound!" That was exactly the thing NOT to say. "I am an old orchestrator and it DOES sound!" replied Ravel. You can imagine the malaise. . . . I could not calm Ravel, who later on opposed Wittgenstein's coming to Paris. Justly furious, the latter wrote to him, "Interpreters do not have to be slaves," and Ravel answered him, "Interpreters *are* slaves!" In fact, Wittgenstein did not play the work in Paris until 1933. It being his exclusive property for six years, it was only in 1937 that it was accessible to others.[6]

The two men eventually patched things up. Ravel had no choice, since the commission granted the pianist exclusive rights to the *Concerto*. Wittgenstein never fully appreciated the masterpiece that had been created for him:

My conviction is the concerti written for me by Labor, Schmidt and R. Strauss (as different as they are from one another) are musically worth more, stand on a higher plane and hence in the end are more durable than Ravel's *Concerto*. I know that such a view may sound paradoxical here in the USA where Labor and Schmidt are completely unknown and Ravel stands at the height of his fame. But I don't err. Let me assure you that I am neither influenced by provincial Austrian patriotism nor personal friendship.[7]

Wittgenstein was quite possessive about his commissions and understandably, for what other music could he play? Franz Schmidt wrote six works for Wittgenstein: three quintets, two pieces for piano and orchestra, and a solo *Toccata*. When Friedrich Wührer, supposedly following a wish expressed by Schmidt on his death-bed, arranged the quintets and concerti for two hands, Wittgenstein, who had paid handsomely for the one-hand settings, was furious. There followed a bitter exchange of letters with Schmidt's widow.

The debate raised an interesting question. Wührer claimed that his arrangements for two hands were new, independent works. Wittgenstein disagreed, insisting that one could "arrange" a two-hand work for one hand, but not the other way around. In any case, a compromise was reached: the new versions could be published, but only if every concert program explained that the works had been originally written for the left hand for Paul Wittgenstein and that these new arrangements had been made with his permission.

Wittgenstein received some glowing reviews for his American performances of Britten and Ravel, and his solo programs were ambitious. His New York recital in Town Hall, in November 1944, featured Wittgenstein's own very difficult arrangement of the "Liebestod" from Wagner's *Tristan und Isolde* (see Ex.16). He also played three Chopin/Godowsky *Paraphrases*, which require great courage. Wittgenstein left two recordings, and it is painful to report that they are, in a word, awful. His renderings of the Ravel *Concerto* and Strauss's *Parergon*, together with the Bach *Chaconne* and other transcriptions, are totally lacking in refinement. The sound is harsh, the pedaling poor. One might give him the benefit of the doubt in that the recordings were made late in his career. However, conductor Trevor Harvey, who was a great personal friend, says that when he knew Wittgenstein in Vienna in the 1930s, "the nervous intensity that he developed led him often to play insensitively and loudly and not always with great accuracy."[8] Indeed, when young Paul still had both arms Leschetizky inscribed a portrait of himself to his pupil "in friendly remembrance of Theodor Leschetizky to his dear pupil Paul Wittgenstein, the mighty string smasher, Vienna, June 26th, 1913."[9]

EX. 16. **Wagner/Wittgenstein: "Liebestod," from *Tristan und Isolde* (Universal, 1957), mm. 35–38.**

Wittgenstein fled Vienna just before the Nazi takeover. He settled in New York City, where he remained, performing and teaching, for the last 23 years of his life. At the end of his career he published his three-volume *School for the Left Hand*, which contains many of his transcriptions, as well as a plethora of interesting and truly finger-twisting exercises.

Despite the shortcomings of Wittgenstein's playing, we can remember a fascinating and courageous man. How many musicians would try to go on being pianists after losing an arm? The cruel trick Fate played on Wittgenstein resulted in some fine music by Schmidt, Britten, and others, as well as one definite masterpiece—the *Concerto* in D by Ravel.

The life of Wittgenstein inspired a picaresque novel by John Barchilon entitled *The Crown Prince* (New York: W. W. Norton, 1984). The name of the hero is real, but the musical events are wildly implausible.

Wittgenstein's career makes one wonder about the many other pianists who lost an arm in wartime. It is no coincidence that Zichy and Wittgenstein, the two players to achieve wide fame and success, came from families of great wealth and the highest social standing. How many shattered hopes will we never know of, how many anonymous lives were left unfulfilled?

Notes

1. Survey of the Literature

1. Faubion Bowers, *Scriabin: A Biography of the Russian Composer 1871–1915* (Tokyo and Palo Alto: Kodansha International Ltd., 1969), p. 155.

2. *Letters of Clara Schumann and Johannes Brahms 1853–1896,* 2 vols., edited by Berthold Litzmann (New York: Longmans, Green and Co., 1927; reprint, New York: Vienna House, 1974).

3. Interview with Carol Montparker, *Clavier,* 25/8 (October 1986):10.

4. William Mason, *Memories of a Musical Life* (New York: AMS Press, 1970; reprinted from the 1901 edition), p. 256.

5. Jeremy Nicholas, *Godowsky: the Pianist's Pianist* (Hexham, Northumberland: Appian Publications & Recordings, 1989), p. 37.

6. Halsey Stevens, *Life and Music of Béla Bartók* (London and New York: Oxford University Press, 1953), pp. 17–18.

7. Nicholas, p. 63.

8. Harold Schonberg, *The Great Pianists* (New York: Simon and Schuster, 1963), p. 339.

9. "Leopold Godowsky—An Appreciation of him as Man, Composer and Pianist," *The Musical Courier,* 1906. Quoted in Nicholas, p. 50.

10. *Grove's Dictionary of Music and Musicians,* 5th ed., edited by Eric Blom (New York: St. Martin's Press, 1954), article "Henri Herz."

11. Arthur Loesser, *Men, Women and Pianos: A Social History* (New York: Simon and Schuster, 1954), p. 361.

12. Peter Ostwald, *Schumann: The Inner Voices of a Musical Genius* (Boston: Northeastern University Press, 1985), p. 122.

13. Heinrich Heine, *Lutezia: Berichte über Politik, Kunst und Volksleben,* Zweiter Teil, vol. 9 of Sämtliche Werke (Leipzig: Insel-Verlag, 1910), Paris, March 20, 1843, p. 271.

2. Alexander Dreyshock

1. Mason, pp. 66–67.

2. *Revue et gazette musicale,* May 19, 1839, p. 200.

3. Ibid., February 12, 1843, p. 55.

4. Heine, *Lutezia,* p. 344; Paris, March 26, 1843.

5. *The Memoirs of Hector Berlioz* (London: Gollancz, 1969), p. 379.

6. Letter of March 27, 1853, in *The Early Correspondence of Hans von Bülow,* edited by his widow, translated by Constance Bach (London: T. Fisher Unwin, 1896).

7. *The Times of London,* April 25, 1843.

8. Ibid., May 13, 1843.

9. *Recent Music and Musicians as described in the Diary and Correspondence of Ignaz Moscheles,* edited by his wife, Charlotte Moscheles, translated by A.D. Coleridge (New York: Henry Holt & Co., 1873).

10. Mason, p. 66.

3. Adolfo Fumagalli

1. *Revue et gazette musicale,* May 13, 1849, pp. 148–49.

2. Ibid., March 7, 1852, p. 77.

3. Ibid., January 7, 1855, p. 35.

4. Filippo Filippi, *Delle vita e delle opere di Adolfo Fumagalli* (Milan: Ricordi, c. 1858), p. 65.

5. Ibid., p. 56.

6. *Constitutionnel,* February 13, 1855.

7. *Revue et gazette musicale,* October 14, 1855, p. 321.

8. *L'Indépendence Belge,* quoted in Filippi, p. 73.

9. Ibid.

4. Geza Zichy

1. Geza Zichy, *Aus meinem Leben: Erinnerungen und Fragmente* (Stuttgart: Deutsche Verlagsanstalt, 1911), p. 82.

2. Ibid., p. 80.

3. Ibid., p. 81.

4. Ibid., p. 85.

5. Ibid., p. 122.

6. *The Letters of Franz Liszt to Olga von Meyendorff 1871–1886 in the Mildred Bliss Collection at Dumbarton Oaks,* translated by William R. Tyler (Cambridge and London: Harvard University Press, 1979), p. 337.

7. Quoted in 71/1 Arthur M. Abell, "Count Geza Zichy," *The Musical Courier* (July 17, 1915).

8. *Liszt/Meyendorff Letters,* p. 421.

5. Paul Wittgenstein

1. Joseph Wechsberg, "His Hand touched our hearts," *Coronet* 25/8 (June 1959):25.

2. Paul Wittgenstein, *Über einarmiges Klavierspiel* (New York: The Austrian Institute, 1958).

3. E. Fred Flindell, "Paul Wittgenstein: Patron and Pianist," *Music Review* 32/2 (May 1971):119.

4. Letter of September 11, 1931, quoted in Flindell, pp. 119–20.

5. Trevor Harvey, "Paul Wittgenstein," *The Gramophone,* June 1961, p. 2.

6. Marguerite Long, *Au piano avec Maurice Ravel* (Paris: Juillard, 1971), p. 59.

7. Quoted in Flindell, p. 123.

8. Harvey, p. 2.

9. Quoted in Flindell, p. 111.

Part Two

CATALOGUE

6.

Solo Works for the Left Hand Alone

Hans Abrahamsen (b 1952). Danish
October (1969; revised 1976). Copenhagen: Wilhelm Hansen.

Jean Absil (b Bon-Secours, Haincaut, 1893; d Brussels, 1974). Belgian organist and composer, professor at Brussels Conservatory.
Ballade, op. 129. Brussels: Centre Belge de Documentation Musicale, 1972. A major work, wide-ranging in mood and tempo, with a declamatory opening and an exciting finish. Well written in a conservative contemporary harmonic idiom dominated by the augmented triad. Trills, thirds, and octaves. D.

Yvonne Adair
Three Preludes. London: Joseph Williams, Ltd., 1930. Gavotte-like. Good for children, M-E. L of C.

Mrs. Crosby Adams (b. Niagara Falls, 1858)
Studies, op. 7. Chicago: C.F. Summy, 1900. E.

Frank Adlam
Triumph Impromptu. London: Nightingale & Co., 1918. Tonal. M-D. NYPL, L of C.

Barbara Lee Agee (b 1932)
Ascent. Unpublished ms., 1950. M-D. L of C.

John Carver Alden
Gavotte. Boston: B.F. Wood, 1904. A catchy main theme, marred by too many broken chords. 7 pp. M-D. NYPL, L of C.

Maisie Aldridge
The Bass Clef Book. London: Augener; New York: Gallaxy Music Corp., 1965. Simple
   tunes for beginners. E. L of C.

Charles Valentin Alkan (b Paris 1813; d Paris 1888). French pianist and composer of
monstrously difficult and very long piano works. A recluse, Alkan almost never performed in public, though his legendary technique was admired by fellow-Parisians
Chopin and Liszt. With very few exceptions, pianists have ignored his vast musical
oeuvre.
Fantaisie in A-flat, op. 76 no. 1. Gerard Billaudot Editions Musicales, 1846. In "Lewenthal." One of three works in op. 76 (the others are études for the right hand alone
   and for two hands), this is one of the first virtuoso works for the left hand. According
   to Raymond Lewenthal, prominent Alkan scholar, it was written around 1838.
     Through thematic transformation, the dignified opening motives serve as
   musical material for the fast finale. The *Fantaisie* is fraught with hair-raising difficulties and fistfuls of chords; unfortunately, the paucity of melody, the
   simple-minded progressions, and some monotonous textures leave an empty impression. Requires excellent tremolos. 10 pp.
     Alkan's *Etude,* op. 35 no. 8, in A-flat, is a three-in-one study. Not strictly for
   left hand alone, it contains a lyrical section for left-hand solo, one for right-hand
   solo, and finally both hands combined.

Louis Andriessen (b Utrecht, 1939). Dutch
Trois pieces, 1961. In *6 Pieces for Left Hand by Dutch Composers.* Amsterdam: Donemus,
   1963. I. *Promenade.* Slow, with an interesting alternation of *pedale* and *senza pedale*
   effects; a good piece. II. *Fracas.* A toccata. Dry, dissonant, martellato; meter shifts,
   M-D. III. *Hymne.* Very slow moving dissonant chords; not easy to sustain interest
   in performance. Large hand required.

Willem Andriessen (b Haarlem, 1887; d Amsterdam, 1964). Dutch pianist and composer, director of the Amsterdam Conservatory.
Preludium (1960). In *6 Pieces for Left Hand by Dutch Composers.* Amsterdam: Donemus,
   1963. An impressively rich and sonorous mood piece, with fine voicing that often
   sounds like two hands (see Ex.17). Contrasting middle section. Good music, despite the jarring last measures.

EX. 17. **Andriessen:** *Preludium* (**Donemus, 1960**), mm. 24–27.

Pierre Augiéras
25 Studies. New York: G. Schirmer, 1917. A set of one- and two-page pieces, each with a fairly difficult technical pattern; of slight interest. L of C.

Carl Philipp Emanuel Bach (b Weimar, 1714; d Hamburg, 1788). The second son of J.S. Bach, renowned as a keyboard player. The clavichord was his specialty, and according to Grove's *Dictionary* he was left-handed.
Klavierstück in A for one hand. Helm #241, Wotquenne 117/1. Written before 1770. In *Kleine Stücke für Klavier,* edited by O. Vrieslander, Hanover, 1930; also in "Lewenthal." The earliest known work for one hand, certainly written for a child. Very short basic patterns in single notes (see Ex.18).

EX. 18. C.P.E. Bach: *Klavierstück*, mm. 1–4.

Freda Bailey. English piano teacher who, according to the Disabled Living Foundation, has written and arranged some of her own music for one-handed pianists.
Nocturne for a Left Hand Performer (and other works).

Zeqirja Ballata. Yugoslavian
Dve Skladbi za klavir (2 pieces for piano). Ljubljana: Drustvo Slovenskih Skladateljev, 1970. To Tatjana Bučar. 1. *Echi delle Montagne Maledette: Andante con variazioni.* 2. *Fantasia rustica.* Both use quartal harmony and reveal the influence of Bartók. 9 pp. University of Wisconsin at Milwaukee.

Béla Bartók (b Nagyszentmiklos, Hungary, 1881; d New York, 1945)
Etude in B-flat (1903). Boosey & Hawkes; Editio Musica Budapest; Kalmus; Dover Bartók Vol. I; "Lewenthal." Dedicated to his teacher István Thoman, the Etude is a fine example of Bartók's early style. It still bore the title *Sonata* when Bartók played the première in Budapest, but the other movements were never written. At 22, he was a concert artist in the Romantic tradition: Liszt was his idol and remained so. Another early influence was Richard Strauss. One of Bartók's stunts was a performance, from memory, of the *Heldenleben* and there are echoes of Strauss in the opening "call to action" (see Ex.10, p. 13). Despite a few awkward harmonic turns and a sectional feeling to the form, this is a very strong piece, wide-ranging in mood. The tender second theme could almost be by Brahms (see Ex.19a). The difficulties are of accuracy rather than speed—excellent octaves are required (see Ex.19b). It is no surprise to learn that Bartók scored a great success with this piece both in his native city and at his Berlin debut. 10 min. D.

Arnold Bax (b Streatham, 1883; d Cork, 1953). British
Slow Movement of the Left Hand Concertante. Chappell. A solo arrangement from Bax's *Concertante* for piano left hand and orchestra.

EX. 19. Bartók: *Etude* (Kalmus, c. 1904?). a. mm. 32–42;
b. development section, mm. 80–82.

Richard Owen Beachcroft
Air and Variations. London: Oxford University Press, 1917. 13 pp. D. L of C.

Karl Beecher
4 Präludien. Berlin: Schlesinger, 1928.

Berenice Bentley (b Iowa, 1887; d California, 1971)
A Happy Heart; Just a-foolin'; Prince Fairy Foot; Vagrant Breeze. C.F. Summy Co., 1944.
Four easy pieces for children. L of C.

Hermann Berens (b Hamburg, 1826; d Stockholm, 1880). Composer/pianist who settled in Sweden at age 21 and became the queen's piano teacher.
Die Pflege der linken Hand (The Training of the Left Hand), op. 89. C.F. Peters, 1872. 46
exercises and 25 studies. The exercises contain scale figures, thirds, and various
broken chords (see Ex.20a). More important are the studies, half-page, self-contained musical works covering an impressive range of techniques and tempos.
Very conservative harmonically, of substantial technical merit and not without eloquence (see Ex.20b). Except for the broken octaves, the Berens pieces are within
the range of a good younger student. A valuable collection.

Francesco Berger (b 1834; d London, 1933). British pianist, student of Plaidy, and
teacher at the Royal Academy. His memoirs are titled 97—they were written at that age.
Six Bagatelles. London: Augener, 1921. Well-crafted short teaching pieces. Though they
move a single note at a time, they convey the national characteristics implicit in
the titles: Spain, Scotland, Italy, etc. E. L of C.

EX. 20. Berens (C.F. Peters, 1872). a. *Exercise* no. 11;
b. *Etude* no. 9, mm. 1–4.

Ludwig Berger (b Berlin, 1777; d Berlin, 1839). German composer and pianist active in St. Petersburg and later in Berlin. He taught Mendelssohn and influenced his piano writing (e.g., *Songs Without Words*). In 1817 his career was curtailed by a nervous disorder of the arm.
> *Etudes,* op. 12 (1820). No. 9 in G major. In "Lewenthal" and Peters/Ruthardt. Probably the first published composition specifically for the left hand alone. It is no surprise to learn that Schumann admired Berger's op. 12: it has some of his dreamy, inward quality. This is an expressive study, not hard, with a *minore* middle section.

Ralph Berkowitz (b New York City, 1910). Dean of the Berkshire Center from 1947.
> *The Right Hand's Vacation: Five Pieces for the Left Hand Alone.* Philadelphia: Elkan-Vogel, 1952. *Tuning Up; Two Sad Clowns; The Harp; Spanish Dance; Circus March.* Short easy works for children.

Maurice Besly
> *Eidulion, Piece for One Piano Left Hand Alone,* op. 29 no. 3. Rogers.

Carl Bial
> 4 *Clavier-Stücke,* op. 30. Berlin, 1884. Brit. Lib.

Mathilde Bilbro (b Tuskegee, Alabama, 1880). Composer of theater works and 300 pieces of sheet music.
> *Melody in D-flat.* White-Smith Publications, 1912. Rather simple, well-written "parlor" music. L of C.

Ludvig Harboe Gote Birkedal-Barford (1850–1937). Danish
> *Exercises,* op. 8 (called *Studien* in the original edition). 15 technically useful pieces, of which no. 8 is outstanding. L of C.
> *Melodic Studies,* op. 19. Copenhagen: Wilhelm Hanson, 1902. 5 lyrical pieces, moderate difficulty and of little musical value. L of C.

Emile R. Blanchet (b Lausanne, 1877; d Pully, near Lausanne, 1943). Swiss composer/pianist, student of Busoni, a teacher at the Lausanne Conservatory. He wrote almost all his music for the piano. An internationally known mountain climber, he scaled several peaks for the first time and wrote two books on the subject.

13 Etudes, op. 53. Paris: Eschig, 1932. Dedicated to Rudolph Ganz. A major collection, Blanchet's *Etudes* present a real problem. The writing is extremely resourceful, with no end of counterpoint, double notes, and clever patterns (it was Blanchet who received the dedication of Godowsky's thorny *Etude Macabre*), but as music it has limited appeal. The harmony is curiously neutral and arbitrary, and the pieces lack formal direction. Nevertheless, pianists and composers will want to examine this music as a fine example of the textural possibilities in one-hand piano writing. 37 pp. D.

64 Preludes, op. 41. Paris: Eschig, 1926. Book 4 is for left hand.

Exercises pour la main gauche seule. Schott.

Allan Blank (b New York City, 1925). American composer and violinist.

Six Studies for Piano One Hand (Left or Right), Set 1, 1992. *Limited Shapes; Around Sustained Tones; Contrasts; Riding the Beat; Semi-Improvisation* (without bar-lines); *Serious Events.* Fast staccatos and passage-work. 17 pp. D.

Six Studies for One Hand, Set 2 (1993). For left hand: II. *Dirge;* IV. *Pantaloon's Dance;* VI. *Determination.* (I, III, and V are for the right hand.) Both sets available from American Composers Editions, 170 W. 74 St., New York, NY 10023.

Paul Bliss (b Chicago, 1872; d New York, 1933). Organist and music editor in Oswego, NY.

Three Fancies. Boston: B.F. Wood, 1925. *In Lilac Time; A Summer Reverie; By Quiet Water.* Fairly easy teaching pieces in salon style. L of C.

Felix Blumenfeld (b Kovalyovka, Ukraine, 1863; d Moscow, 1931). Prominent Russian conductor, pianist, composer, and teacher. He was the uncle of Heinrich Neuhaus and counted among his pupils Vladimir Horowitz. After studies with Rimsky-Korsakoff he taught at the St. Petersburg Conservatory, conducted in Paris, and gave the first performances of many piano works by Glazunov, Lyadov, and Arensky.

Etude in A-flat, op. 36. Leipzig: Belaieff, 1905. In "Lewenthal." Dedicated to Leopold Godowsky after the latter's stunning successes in Russia. This gem of a melody has a clever accompaniment weaving above and below it (see Ex.21a); there is a "pathetic" middle section (Ex.21b), and an effective cadenza. The return veers toward sentimentality but the over-all effect remains strong. M-D.

Carlotta Bocca

Ten Melodious Compositions, op. 20. Boston: B.F. Wood, 1925. Good progressions, well laid-out for the hand; some challenge for a young person. Dated in style, but *Arabesque, Burlesque,* and *Nocturne* are recommended. L of C.

Ferdinando Bonamici (b Naples, 1827; d Naples, 1905). Italian pianist and composer, teacher at Naples Conservatory. He organized the first Italian musical congresses and was helpful in raising the level of culture in his country.

100 Exercices et 153 Passages divers, op. 271.

30 Exercices-Etudes, op. 272.

EX. 21. **Blumenfeld:** *Etude* (Belaieff, 1905). a. mm. 1–4;
b. mm. 31–32.

34 *Etudes Mélodiques,* op. 273. Paris: Société anonyme des éditions Ricordi, 1915. In an
introduction to this reprint, Isidor Philipp calls the vast collection "remarkable
and the most complete work for the left hand alone." No one could argue with its
completeness—the numbers speak for themselves. Op. 271 is excellent, with
scores of useful exercises (see Ex.22a). Bonamici was not a first-class composer,
and in op. 273 he ran into trouble trying to bring musical values to the fore. Op.
272 contains a good study in double notes (Ex.22b).

EX. 22. **Bonamici (Ricordi, 1915). a.** *Exercice* no. 4; b. *Exercice-Etude*
no. 21, mm. 1–3.

Capriccio sull' Opera La Straniera de Bellini, op. 96. Milan: G. Ricordi, c. 1865.

Frederic Bontoft
Prelude and Fughetta. London: Augener, 1958. The *Prelude* is in neo-Baroque style, a
toccata-like allegro in D minor. The *Fughetta* is barely contrapuntal, except one
fine spot toward the end, where the subjects of both pieces are combined. 6 pp.
M-D. L of C.

Sergei Eduardovich Bortkiewicz (b Kharkov, 1877; d Vienna, 1952). Austrian com-
poser/pianist of Russian origin. He scored a great success with his first piano concerto
and wrote a second for the left hand alone on a commission from fellow-Viennese Paul
Wittgenstein.
Etude in F-sharp, Le Poète. No. 5, from *12 Etudes nouvelles,* op. 29. Leipzig: D. Rahter,
1924. Mellifluous lyricism, showing the influence of Scriabin. M-D. NYPL.

Charles Samuel Bovy-Lysberg (b Geneva, 1821; d Geneva, 1873). One of Chopin's best
students in Paris; Liszt arranged for the publication of his op. 1.
Etude, op. 20. Paris: Richault, c. 1848.

York Bowen (1884–1961). British. According to Maurice Hinson, "Bowen was a fine pianist and wrote a great deal for the piano. His pedagogical editions are highly regarded
in Great Britain."
Nocturne from *Curiosity Suite,* op. 42. London: J. Williams, 1916. This is the fifth movement of an eight-movement suite written mostly for two hands (the *Caprice* is for
right hand alone). The *Nocturne* is a *Grave* in F minor, declamatory and Romantic. 4 pp. M-D. L of C, NYPL.

Harold de Bozi
Tango. New York: Associated Music Publishers.

Theodore Vaclav (Wenzel Theodore) Bradsky (b Rakovnik, 1833; d Rakovnik, 1881).
Bohemian musician and court composer to King Georg of Prussia.
La petite Fadette: Morceau de Concert, op. 22. Berlin: Stempelman, c. 1862.

Johannes Brahms (b Hamburg, 1833; d Vienna, 1897)
Chaconne from the *Partita* No. 2 in D minor for solo violin, BWV 1016, by J.S. Bach.
Leipzig: B. Senff, 1879. Available separately from Ricordi, Simrock, and Breitkopf
& Härtel. The last of *Five Studies* (without opus number), all transcriptions of
music by other composers. The other works in this group are for two hands, with
very difficult left-hand parts. Brahms was a good pianist, although as the Viennese critic Eduard Hanslick wrote, he sounded like someone who has more
important things to do than practice five hours a day. Brahms had his didactic
side and took a lively interest in piano technique: one thinks of the *Paganini Variations,* worked out with pianist Carl Tausig, and the *51 Exercises.* Perhaps he
inherited an interest in the left hand from his teacher (see Eduard Marxsen)—
certainly many of his piano scores contain extraordinary left-hand challenges.
    The *Chaconne* was written down for Brahms's close friend Clara Schumann
(see also p. 7, above):

> I don't suppose I have ever sent you anything as amusing as what I am sending you today, provided your fingers can survive the pleasure! . . . I only wrote it for you. But do not overstrain your hand; it requires so much resonance and strength. Play it for a while *mezza voce*. Also make the fingering easy and convenient. If it does not exert you too much—which is what I am afraid of—you ought to get great fun out of it. Portschach, June, 1877.

Clara responded:

> It was indeed a most wonderful surprise I found awaiting me here! Just think, wasn't it strange, on the day after my arrival here, when I was opening a drawer I strained a muscle in my right hand, so you may imagine what a glorious refuge your Chaconne has been to me! You alone could have accomplished such a thing, and what seems to me most extraordinary about it is the way in which you so faithfully reproduce the sound of the violin. However you came to think of it amazes me. It is true my fingers do not altogether master it . . . and my right hand itches to join in. But for this, I do not find the difficulties insuperable, and the pleasure I get is enormous. Kiel, July 6. [From *Letters of Clara Schumann and Johannes Brahms 1853–1986*, edited by Berthold Litzmann (New York: Vienna House, 1973), Vol. II, pp. 16–17.]

Although one often reads that Brahms arranged the *Chaconne* for Clara because she had injured her right hand, their exchange of letters clearly shows that the timing was only a fortunate coincidence. Clara rather overstates Brahms's accomplishment when she says he "reproduces the sound of the violin." He has simply moved the piece down an octave, with 99 percent of the details intact (see Exx.23a and b).

The *Chaconne* transcription is faithful to the point of severity, and its makes an interesting comparison with Busoni's famous arrangement for two hands. Where Brahms left the harmony implied, Busoni has filled it out (see Exx.23c and d).

Bach's rhythm and melody are rendered with special care, though there are some enrichments of texture. Most interesting are the performance indications for phrasing and dynamics, revealing Brahms as a superb editor of early music. He was gratified by Clara's response and wrote back in July 1877: "Let me thank you again for your kind letter. I am delighted that the *Chaconne* was not merely a childish freak, and that it gave you pleasure and everything." Brahms was often self-deprecating when writing to Clara, at times dismissing significant masterpieces as "trifles."

Rudolf Braun (1869–1925) [according to NYPL, d Vienna, 1957]. Blind organ virtuoso, teacher of composition in Vienna.
3 Klavierstücke. Vienna: Doblinger 1928. *Scherzo; Perpetuum mobile; Serenata*. Written for Paul Wittgenstein in 1922.
3 Klavierstücke. Doblinger, 1928. *Nocturno; À la zingarese; Walzer*. Tonal, very conservative harmony for the period; well written for the hand, but musically insignificant. The *Perpetuum mobile* is a useful drill.

Thérèse Brenet (b Paris, 1935). French pianist and composer, professor at the Paris Conservatoire.
Oceanides: étude pour main gauche. Paris: Henry Lemoine, 1988. 9 pp. Northwestern University.

EX. 23. a. Bach: *Chaconne* for violin (Bärenreiter, 1955), mm. 22–29;
b. Bach/Brahms: *Chaconne* (Breitkopf & Härtel, 1926,) mm. 22–29;
c. Bach/Busoni: *Chaconne* (Breitkopf & Härtel, 1893), mm. 81–82;
d. Bach/Brahms: *Chaconne* (Breitkopf & Härtel, 1926), mm. 81–82.

Walter Bricht (b Vienna, 1904; d Bloomington, IN, 1970). In United States from 1938, later a professor at Indiana University. The following pieces, all written for Paul Wittgenstein, were never published.
Fantasy on motives from Gounod's Faust (c. 1936).
Fantasy on Themes of Die Fledermaus.
Lied ohne Worte; Albumblatt; Perpetuum mobile (c. 1937).

Frank Bridge (b Brighton, 1879; d Eastbourne, 1941). British composer, violist, and conductor; teacher of Benjamin Britten.

Three Improvisations. London: W. Rogers, 1919. The first two, *At Dawn* and *A Vigil,* are rather easy, and are written in a reflective style. The third, *A Revel,* is in fast triplets—effective. All solidly constructed. 8 pp. M-D. NYPL.

Colin Brumbry (b Melbourne, 1933). Teacher at Queensland University.
Reverie. In "Australian." A whimsical waltz in a conservative idiom; for youngsters.

Sas Bunge (1924–1980) Dutch
10 Etudes. Amsterdam: Donemus, 1977. Photo of ms. Ten short studies—one page each—in a dry, conservative style; key signatures. M-D. Harvard University.

Hans Bussmeyer (b Braunschweig, 1853). A student of Liszt.
Minuetto, Fughetta und Burletta. Munich: Schmid, c. 1885.

Maria Buttner
6 *Osterreichische Tänze* (left or right hand alone). Vienna: Doblinger, 1946. Melodious *Ländler,* high quality music for young people. In an Afterword Buttner dedicated her pieces to the soldiers wounded in World War II. NYPL.

Curt Cacciopo
Beloved Emblem: Left Hand Study for the Piano. Bryn Mawr: Orenda Press, 1983. 3 pp. Haverford College.

Elsa Calcagno (b Buenos Aires, 1916). Argentinian
12 Preludios (6 para la mano izquierda). Buenos Aires: Ricordi. Fairly simple pieces, some with a feeling of the tango and other dances. L of C.
Variaciónes clasicos sobre un temade la lianura. Ricordi, 1942.

Gian Paolo Chiti. Italian, born in Rome. Professor of Composition and Deputy Director of the Santa Cecilia Conservatory.
Prelude and Fugue (1993). *Prelude* is fantasy-like with shifting tempos, no barlines; *Fugue* is a two-voice *Andante* that requires a large hand. 8 pp. ms. available from the composer: Via Proba Petronia, 82, Rome 00136.

Ove Christensen (1856–1909). A major Danish pianist of the Romantic period, he spent time at the imperial court in St. Petersburg.
3 Etüden. Leipzig and Boston: A.P. Schmidt, 1907. Short and rather difficult sixteenth-note studies. No. 1 is especially good for the weak fingers. L of C.

Willem Coenen (b Rotterdam, 1837; d Lugano, 1918). Toured America as pianist but finally settled in London to teach in 1862.
Fantasia on the Last Rose of Summer and God Save the Queen. London, 1864. Brit. Lib.

Felix de Cola (b Capetown, South Africa, 1906). Composer, author, and entertainer. He gave piano lessons to Harpo Marx and invented music systems for the blind.
Left Hand—Right Foot. Summy-Birchard, 1961. Nine brief and easy teaching pieces. Transcriptions of five folk songs and a few tunes by Haydn, Liszt, and Gounod.
Transcriptions: Beethoven's *Minuet in G;* Chopin's *Preludes* in A major and C minor; Lehar's *Merry Widow Waltz. Clavier* 6/3 (March 1967). Includes advice on arranging music for left hand.

John Corigliano (b New York City, 1938). Composer and professor at Lehman College, City University of New York.

Etude-Fantasy (1976). New York: G. Schirmer, 1981. Of the five pieces in this lengthy work only the first is for left hand alone. The composer explained its genesis:

> I wrote Etude-Fantasy in 1976 as part of the bicentennial piano competitions at the Kennedy Center. It was written for James Tocco. The previous season, I heard Tocco's Tully Hall recital, and he played an etude for the left hand by Blumenfeld as an encore. I was fascinated by it, and wanted to experiment in writing for left hand (especially Mr. Tocco's super-virtuosic left hand). . . . This, combined with my desire to write a large-scale Fantasy led to the combination of Etudes and the Fantasy form which resulted in the Etude-Fantasy. [letter to the author.]

The opening, a clangorous recitative— "stark and fierce"—is followed by a slower, legato theme marked "icy." The transition to the second *Etude* is effective, with the right hand creeping in *pianissimo* at the top of the piano; of course, this linking of the two makes it impossible to perform the first *Etude* independently. The final section is a lyric reminiscence on the opening themes. The left-hand piece is of moderate difficulty and effectively explores different possibilities of ornamentation and touch.

Caroline H. Crawford

A Summer Shower: A Study of Broken Octaves, op. 5. Boston: B.F. Wood, 1919. Six pages of perpetual motion. M-D. NYPL.

Mentor Crosse, editor

Standard Studies for the Left Hand in Seven Volumes. Cincinnati: John Church Co., 1918. An immense, unprecedented collection of approximately a thousand pages of music, but almost all of it is for two hands with a challenging left-hand part, arranged in order of progressive difficulty. The actual music for left hand alone are the preparatory exercises in each volume, Greulich's *Etudes* in F-sharp minor and B minor (Vol. V), adaptations of Rubinstein's E-flat major *Etude* and works by Kessler and Chopin, and an untitled piece by Zichy (Vol. VII). L of C.

Carl Czerny (b Vienna, 1791; d Vienna, 1857). Master teacher and one of the most prolific piano composers in history. Czerny taught up to ten hours a day and used four desks when he was writing music; as the ink dried on one score he worked at the next. Czerny was very close to Beethoven—he gave early performances of his music and knew the 32 Sonatas from memory. As a teacher, Czerny has our gratitude for taking in a child of phenomenal but unbridled talent, the nine-year-old Franz Liszt, and teaching him free of charge for two years. A relentless drillmaster, Czerny laid the foundations for Liszt's future achievements. His pupil remained grateful, vowing never to charge a fee for lessons himself.

2 Etudes, op. 735. Vienna: Mechetti, 1846. New edition, Amsterdam: rev. by A.J. Heuwekemeijer, 1969. The opening of No. 1, in G minor, *maestoso,* bears an amusing resemblance to Beethoven's *Choral Fantasy.* The later sections are technically challenging. No. 2, in A-flat major, begins like a Beethoven slow movement, becoming increasingly elaborate. If only it were possible to write in the style of Beethoven,

Czerny would have managed it. But as his music stands, the lack of harmonic variety can be frustrating, particularly in these works, where he aims for greater scope than usual.

Etude for One Hand in A major. In "Lewenthal." Ten very short studies rolled into one fantasy-like composition. The melodic interest is minimal in this pyrotechnical work-out. Although Czerny evidently imagined the *Etude* played by either hand, some passages fairly comfortable for the right are extremely knotty for the left.

Giusto Dacci (b Parma, 1840; d Parma, 1915)
Melodia. Trieste: Schmidl & Co., c. 1894.

C. C. Dean
Il Penseroso, op. 45, no. 16, by Stephen Heller. Chicago: Clayton F. Summy Co., 1916.
A good arrangement of a decent piano piece written originally for two hands; *Andantino.* L of C.

Joseph Dichler (b Vienna, 1912). Pianist, teacher at the Academy of Music and author of a book on piano playing.
Intermezzo and Capriccio. Vienna: Doblinger, 1980. Dichler's style is tonally conservative, almost jazzy in places (see Ex.24).

EX. 24. **Dichler:** *Intermezzo* **(Doblinger, 1980), mm. 1–9.**

The *Capriccio* is a strong polonaise. Literal quotations from Chopin and Rachmaninoff are marked "inner voices." The score calls for "smashing" by the hand, fist, and arm. One of the best contemporary left-hand works. 16 pp. M-D.

Edward B. Dickinson
Kathleen Mavourneen, op. 15. New York: A.G. Slade, 1881. One of the most elaborate and lengthy transcriptions; pyrotechnics, some awkward writing. 12 pp. L of C.

Ernst von Dohnányi (b Pozsony, now Bratislava, 1877; d New York City, 1960). One of Hungary's foremost twentieth-century musicians—a composer, conductor, administrator, and first-class pianist. He had a vast repertoire, gave many pioneering concerts, and in later years taught in the United States.
Fugue (1913). New York: Associated, 1962. Bearing the subtitle "for one advanced left

hand or two unadvanced hands," this is a true fugue in a rather chromatic D minor. The exposition introduces four real voices. Later the texture becomes free, and inversions, stretti, and augmentation are introduced. This ambitious work starts quietly, gradually gathering steam. Large hand required for the final trill. M-D.

Alexander Dreyschock (b Žak, 1818; d Venice, 1869). See above, pp. 17–20.

Variationen, op. 22 (sometimes called *Etude,* though not in the original edition). London: R. Cocks & Co.; Paris: Schlesinger, 1843. Dedicated to Charlotte Fink. This pioneering work by the first left-hand player consists of an introduction, a long *Tema* in binary form, and a series of increasingly difficult variations. The harmony is classical and the musical value slight, with some harmonic gaucheries. Dreyschock obviously had a huge hand; the *Variations* are difficult, calling for fast leaps and a knotty trill for the inner fingers. Excellent octaves and thirds are called for (see Ex.25). 12 pp. Cleveland Public Library.

EX. 25. **Dreyschock:** *Variations* (Schlesinger, 1843), mm. 11–13.

Grand Variation sur l'Air God Save the Queen (written before 1854). Offenbach: André, 1862. The theme is given out in wide arpeggios and then filled out with incredibly fast figurations and octave work (see Ex.13)—a true blockbuster.

Percival Driver

Single Handed Pieces. 4 books. London: Boosey & Hawkes.

Hubert Eckartz

Capriccio, from *8 Klavierstücke.* In "Georgii." *Vivo molto,* shifting meters; tonal. M-D.

George Eggeling

Mélodie in F-sharp minor, op. 178. A.P. Schmidt, 1912. L of C, NYPL.

On the Lagoon: Barcarolle, op. 165. Philadelphia: Theodore Presser, 1913. Nicely written, 4 pp. M. L of C.

Selma Epstein. An American pianist specializing in the music of women composers, Epstein has edited a volume of piano works for one and three hands written by women. Catalogue available from Chromatica USA, 2443 Pickwick Rd., Dickeyville, MD 21207.

Heinrich van Eyken (b Elberfeld, 1861; d Berlin, 1908). German active in Berlin, known as a songwriter.
Romanze, op. 8. Berlin: Raabe & Plowthow, c. 1894.

Edmund Eysler (b Vienna, 1874; d Vienna, 1949). A highly successful composer of operettas.
12 Etüden. Wiener Dreiklangverlag, 1946. Well written and fairly simple music for
    children. This small book contains pictures. NYPL.

Jan Felderhof (b Bussum, 1907). Dutch composer and prominent harmony teacher.
Impression (1959). In *6 Pieces for Left Hand by Dutch Composers.* Amsterdam: Donemus,
    1963. A sonorous mood piece, *quasi improvisando,* written for the injured Dutch
    pianist Cor de Groot. Mostly atonal; legato with much pedal. M-D.

William M. Felton (b 1887; d Philadelphia, 1942). Organist.
Solfeggietto, by C.P.E. Bach. Philadelphia: Theodore Presser, 1932. A transcription; sim-
    plified in a few places. L of C.

Wilhelm Fink
Romanze, op. 200, no. 1. Philadelphia: Theodore Presser, 1913. An Adagio in D-flat,
    marred by awkward arpeggios. 4 pp. L of C.

Arthur Foote (b Salem, Mass. 1853; d Boston, 1937). Prominent New England musician, unusual for being entirely American-trained: in 1875 he received from Harvard
University the first master's degree in music awarded in the United States.
A Little Waltz, op. 6, no. 4. Arthur P. Schmidt, 1885. Very modest demands, good for
    children. NYPL.
3 Piano Pieces, op. 37. Arthur P. Schmidt, 1897. I. *Prelude-Etude;* II. *Polka;* III. *Romance.*
    Foote's harmonic vocabulary is practically eighteenth century, and his melodic
    ideas are forgettable, but the *Prelude-Etude* has some real challenges in terms of
    octaves, leaps, and fast scales (see Ex.26).

EX. 26. Foote: *Prelude-Etude* (Arthur P. Schmidt, 1897), mm. 1–3.

Nos. 2 and 3 are rather easy. At the age of 30, Foote went to Europe and studied
the music of Stephen Heller with the composer, later dedicating these three works
to him. L of C.

John Franklyn
Dainty Novellettes. Cincinnati: Willis Co., 1915. 6 short teaching works.
Belfry Echoes; Spring Breezes; In Dewy Gardens (1921).

Dream of an Hour; Forest Glades; In a Snow-clad Vale (1925). L of C.

Adolph Frey (b Landau, 1865; d Syracuse, NY, 1938). German-American pianist, student of Clara Schumann.
Valse Lente. Valse Romantique. Boston: O. Ditson, 1919. Salon music; solidly written and quite easy. L of C.

Berenice Frost
The White Swan. Boston Music Co., 1941.

Adolfo Fumagalli (b Inzago, 1828; d Florence, 1856). In a brief but exciting career, Fumagalli published nearly a hundred piano pieces (see pp. 21–25 for his biography and musical examples). The five for left hand alone are all opera transcriptions and it is good to possess this tangible evidence of his magnificent public successes. (All of Fumagalli's music can be examined at the Verdi Conservatory in Milan.) The strength lies in the basic musical material: it is hard to go wrong with a good tune by Verdi or Bellini. For the most part the writing is clever, occasionally achieving the effect of two hands. The weakness lies in Fumagalli's limited sense of figuration, his adherence to the original orchestral patterns in the accompaniments of lyrical sections, rather than the invention of suitable substitutes. This creates the awkward need to be in two places at once (through very quick arpeggios and broken chords), a problem that cannot be overcome by practice.
Notturno-Studio, op. 2. A student work, probably unpublished.
Studio da Concerto, op. 18, no. 1. Milan: Gio. Canti. The tenor solo from the last scene of Donizetti's *Lucia di Lammermoor.* A literal treatment of the brass introduction with two cadenzas interpolated into the main melody. A great tune with a little too much arpeggiation.
Studio da Concerto: coro nell'opera I Lombardi di Verdi "o Signore! del tetto natìo," op. 18, no. 2. Milan: Gio. Canti. C major, *Adagio,* not too hard, except for an octave glissando at the end. Some awkward spreads; not very appealing musically.
"Casta diva che inargenti" nell'opera Norma di Bellini, op. 61. Milan: G. Ricordi, 1851. Very literal, with two verses, choral interpolations, and a cadenza at the end. This paraphrase gains from its immortal melody (see Ex.27), but it is awkward, requiring, in the first section alone, sixteen breaks between treble and bass. At the repeat, the melody is reinforced with octaves.
Andante nel Mosé (Mi manca la voce), op. 102 posth. Milan: G. Ricordi. Builds up to a very rich texture, but the needlessly literal accompaniment leads to innumerable broken chords.
Grande Fantaisie sur Robert le Diable de Meyerbeer, op. 106. G. Ricordi. Dedicated to Franz Liszt. Long and very difficult; some good writing in which fast and furious octaves, chords, and leaps cover the keyboard (see above Ex.14, p. 23). Least satisfying is the overall form: abrupt and unimaginative transitions link sections which in themselves contain rather thin music. Musically this is the weakest of the transcriptions, though the most ambitious in scope and complexity. 22 pp.

EX. 27. Bellini/Fumagalli: "Casta Diva," from *Norma* (G. Ricordi, 1851), mm. 1–7.

Henri Furlani

Humoresque. Milan: A. and G. Garisch & Co., 1929. Recommended for its perky liveliness and its pianistic challenge. 3 pp. M-D. L of C.

Walter Gage

Impromptu. Philadelphia: M.D. Swisher, 1913. Unmemorable music, too complex for most students because of the swirling arpeggios. L of C.

G. Gaiani

Souvenir de Vienne. c. 1854.

Rudolph Ganz (b Zurich, 1877; d Chicago, 1972). Composer, conductor, and pianist, for many years president of Chicago Musical College. As a pianist he introduced a number of twentieth-century European works to North American audiences.
Capriccio, op. 26, no. 1. New York: G. Schirmer, 1917. (The companion piece is for right hand alone.) 6 pp. M-D. L of C, NYPL.

Harvey Gaul (b New York, 1881; d Pittsburgh, 1945). Studied in Paris with d'Indy. Gaul was active as a conductor/composer in Pittsburgh, where he taught at the Carnegie Institute of Technology.
Bluette Waltz. Boston: C.W. Thompson & Co., 1912. E. L of C.

Walter Georgii, editor (b Stuttgart, 1887; d Tübingen, 1967). Taught at Cologne. His books on piano music include *Geschichte der Musik für Klavier zu 2 Hände,* Zurich, 1941.

The 1950 revised edition contains an essay on music for one, three, and five hands.

Einhändig: Eine Sammlung von originalen and übertragenen Kompositionen für Klavier zu 1 und zu 3 Händen [A collection of original and arranged compositions for 1 and 3 hands]. P. J. Tonger, n.d. The solo works by Bach, Reger, and Scriabin may be found in other editions, but the original solos by Knorr, Zilcher, Ziegler, Petyrek, Maler, Eckartz, and Hoeffer (see under individual composers) are not available elsewhere. For original works for three hands, see below, "Chamber Music." Includes a short essay in German on the left hand literature. Also includes several commissioned pieces for piano and violin. 100 pp.

Heinrich Germer (b Sommersdorf, 1837; d Dresden, 1913). German piano teacher, author of *Die Technik des Klavierspiels.*

25 Stüdien, op. 41. Leipzig: Hug & Co., 1899. A lengthy collection but not difficult enough for real technique building. L of C.

Edwin Gerschefski (b Meriden, CT, 1909). Piano student of Schnabel and prolific composer.

Suite, op. 15 (1934). New York: Pioneer Editions, Inc. *Allegro; Largo; Allegretto; Maestoso.* Atonal; dry textures. 11 pp. 12 min. M-D. American Music Center.

Aurelio Giorni (1895–1938)

Concert-Etude. New York: G. Schirmer, 1918. NYPL (missing).

Francis Goddard

Nocturne. Boston: O. Ditson & Co., 1883. "Parlor" music, easy except for the arpeggiated downbeats. L of C.

Leopold Godowsky (b Vilna, 1870; d New York City, 1938). Fabled virtuoso, revered by his fellow-pianists for the elegant perfection of his technique and his mastery of polyphonic complexities. His playing was the despair of his friends Hofmann and Rachmaninoff, and his students referred to him as "God."

Studies on Chopin's Etudes. 5 vols. Robert Lienau; Berlin: Schlesinger. Consists of 53 Paraphrases, on Chopin's *Etudes,* 22 of them for the left hand alone. Godowsky set all of Chopin's op. 10 for the left hand, most of op. 25, and two of the three posthumous studies. According to Jeremy Nicholas, op. 25, nos. 6, 7, and 8 were also transcribed for left hand but never published—they were "left in Vienna at the outbreak of the First World War, whereabouts unknown" (Nicholas, *Godowsky,* Appendix).

At least ten *Studies* had been written by the year 1893 and performed by Godowsky with sensational effect (see Exx.11 and 12, p. 14); the entire series appeared in print between 1899 and 1914. Isidor Phillip, himself an author of much difficult music for the left hand, wrote: "It is witchcraft, a veritable phantasmagoria! All possible rhythmic combinations are gathered together in this work, and I am convinced that close attention to this extraordinary production will have a great influence on modern pianists." ("Some Recent Music for Piano," *The Etude,* January 1911, p. 162.)

Although we are not directly concerned here with his two-hand music, a quotation from the very first *Study* gives a good idea of the complexity of Godowsky's approach. The left hand must play the very exacting notes originally assigned by Chopin to the right (see Ex.28).

EX. 28. **Chopin/Godowsky:** *Etude*, **op. 10, no. 1, (R. Lienau, 1899–1914), mm. 1–3.**

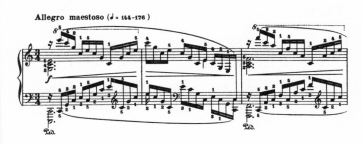

The *Studies* for left hand alone hold a very special place in the repertoire, indeed in the history of piano music. While the overwhelming majority of piano transcriptions stem from vocal and orchestral scores, these are paraphrases of piano music. And what piano music it is! For Chopin's *Etudes* stand at the very summit of works for the instrument. Nevertheless, Godowsky was able to incorporate an unbelievable amount of Chopin's original melodic and harmonic material into the working of a single hand (see Ex.29). Certainly no one had ever written left-hand music of such ingenuity, nor has anyone done so since. Reading through Godowsky's arrangements with *two* busy hands is the best way to appreciate his unique achievement.

EX. 29. **Chopin/Godowsky:** *Etude*, **op. 10, no. 12 (R. Lienau, 1899–1914), mm. 9–12.**

Several *Studies* come with exhaustive preparatory exercises (see Ex.30). Also instructive are the thoughtful pedaling indications and the fingerings, which are of a quality very rarely seen. Godowsky's fingerings resemble the moves of a great chess master who, as a result of deep thought, selects the best from a field of many possibilities.

EX. 30. **Godowsky:** *Preparatory Exercise* to *Etude,* op. 10, no. 2 (**R. Lienau, 1899–1914**).

Godowsky sometimes stays close to Chopin's original, in what he called "strict transcriptions" (see Ex.31). At other times he is a totally creative transcriber, using the original as a springboard for what he termed "free variations." The A minor study begins like Chopin (see Ex.11, p. 14) but uses rhythmic diminution as it proceeds (see Exx.32a and b).

EX. 31. **Chopin/Godowsky:** *Etude,* op. 10, no. 3 (R. Lienau, 1899–1914), mm. 1–4.

EX. 32. **Chopin/Godowsky:** *Etude,* op. 25, no. 4 (R. Lienau, 1899–1914). a. mm. 37–39; b. mm. 45–46.

Since Chopin's basic harmonic progressions are retained and the number of measures is unaltered, the original *Etudes* are always recognizable, despite transpositions, the addition of highly chromatic voices, and even changes in the very purpose of the study. What is questionable are the small—and not-so-small—harmonic additions. In op. 10, no. 3, with the addition of a few appoggiaturas, the "sentiment" in Ex.33a becomes "sentimentality" in Ex.33b. Godowsky can also be accused of upsetting Chopin's perfect structural balance. For example, the original A-flat *Etude* begins very simply, with the telling inner voices entering much later (see Ex.34a). Because Godowsky already forms inner voices by measure 9, the shape of the work is, in a sense, lost (see Ex.34b).

EX. 33. Chopin: *Etude*, op. 10, no. 3, mm. 17–20. a. original version (G. Schirmer, 1916); b. Chopin/Godowksy (R. Lienau, 1899–1914).

EX. 34. Chopin: *Etude*, op. 25, no. 1. a. original version (G. Schirmer, 1916), mm. 17–18; b. Chopin/Godowksy (R. Lienau, 1899–1914), mm. 9–10.

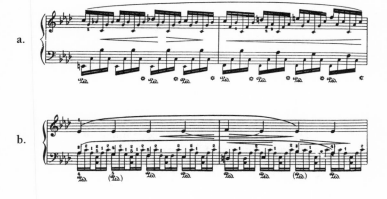

In his "Personal Remarks" Godowsky defended these alterations:

> The original Chopin studies remain as intact now as they were before any arrangements of them were ever published; in fact, the author claims that after assiduously studying the present versions many hidden beauties in the original studies will reveal themselves even to the less observant student.

The immense difficulty of the *Studies* is compounded by highly unusual finger combinations, which the pianist's hand has probably never encountered (see Ex.35); and much of the passagework is without pattern, requiring innumerable repetitions to master and memorize it. Rather than sheer strength, it calls for supreme coordination, as well as fearless accuracy of lateral movement. Significantly, Chopin's thundering octave study became a finger-twister (see Ex.36). Op. 10, no. 2, in particular, is a marvelous drill for the weak fingers (see Ex.37). Artur Rubinstein played it daily.

EX. 35. **Chopin/Godowsky:** *Etude*, **op. 25, no. 12 (R. Lienau, 1899–1914), mm. 1–2.**

EX. 36. **Chopin/Godowsky:** *Etude*, **op. 25, no. 10 (R. Lienau, 1899–1914), mm. 1–2.**

EX. 37. **Chopin/Godowsky:** *Etude*, **op. 10, no. 2 (R. Lienau, 1899–1914), mm. 1–2.**

Four of the Chopin/Godowsky *Studies* are accessible to "mere mortals" as concert repertoire—two of the posthumous works, op. 25, no. 5, and op. 10, no. 6 (the last is shown in Ex.38). The writing here is exceptionally beautiful, and Raymond Lewenthal wisely included it in his Schirmer collection.

Because of their immense difficulty, the *Paraphrases* will never be widely performed, as critic Ernst Taubert predicted in his review of Godowsky's Berlin debut:

Herr Godowsky offered us rare gifts which he had compiled himself out of the studies of Chopin . . . entirely new formations are sounded which moreover nobody will
be able to imitate in playing, because they offer unheard-of technical difficulties which
are only calculated for the abnormal abilities of their author. [Die Post, December
1900.]

That concert proved the turning point of his career, although, having established that glorious career, Godowsky seems not to have played his left-hand
transcriptions. They do not appear on his concert programs, and, with the exception of a single early cylinder (op. 25, nos. 1 and 4), he did not record them.
Godowsky did not even write left-hand music for many years. Was it a strange
kind of prescience that made him return to it at the end of his life? For just after
publishing an extensive series of left-hand works in the late 1920s, Godowsky suffered a stroke which permanently paralyzed his right arm!

EX. 38. Chopin/Godowsky: *Etude*, op. 10, no. 6 (R. Lienau,
1899–1914), mm. 1–2.

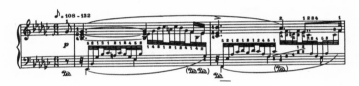

In comparison with the Chopin *Paraphrases,* most of Godowsky's later works
represent a drastic simplification. In a letter to Maurice Aronson, Godowsky expressed great enthusiasm for his recent group of original creations:

My new compositions will please you both, I am sure. They are really inspired—not
composed. Philipp and Blanchet, the only persons who have heard them, are most
enthusiastic—I have a Prelude and Fugue (imagine a real fugue in three voices, inversions, contractions, pedal points and all kinds of devices on B-A-C-H for one
hand!); an Etude "Wailing Winds," an intensely dramatic and gruesome picture; a
poem ("Meditation"), as appealing and tender as "Devotion" or the "Garden," an
Impromptu, Intermezzo and Suite Rococo. [Paris, February 19, 1929; quoted in Nicholas, p. 136.]

In another letter to Aronson, Godowsky continued:

I have developed an uncanny virtuosity in writing for the one hand. . . . You will be
surprised! Besides—all the left-hand pieces are really inspired, not manufactured! I
intend to write a dozen of them in all. Half of them will be short waltzes of my own;
the others will be two Waltz-Paraphrases, the Capriccio, a ballad, a song without
words and a study. Quite an undertaking! The difficulty of the problem attracts me.
They are all polyphonic, contrapuntal, without jumps, without the feeling of compromise and emptiness, in short—one does not miss the right hand and hears at the
same time music, not tricks! [London, June 20, 1928; quoted in Nicholas, p. 135.]

Both Isidor Philipp and Emile Blanchet were outstanding and prolific creators
of left-hand music, and their enthusiasm was inevitable—Godowsky could indeed
claim "an uncanny virtuosity in writing for the one hand." His fifteen late works are

absolute miracles of pianistic invention, continuously producing the effect of two busy hands. But the musical worth is highly debatable. Rachmaninoff's influence is present, though without that master's depth or intensity. And despite mellifluous textures and much chromatic coloring, the melodies are unmemorable, the emotional message rather neutral. Might this be the reason Godowsky's music—including the most playable—has fallen into almost total neglect?

Prelude and Fugue (B.A.C.H.). New York: G. Schirmer, 1930. Dedicated to Arthur Loesser. The *Prelude* is a pastoral *moderato* in F major. The *Fugue,* using a subject based on the notes B.A.C.H. (H in German is B-natural), is a full-fledged structure with stretti, inversions, and a countersubject. The polyphony has a miraculous clarity. Though written in a quick tempo, the *Fugue* is not unplayable. One nice "circular" touch: the *Prelude* ends with a foretaste of the *Fugue* subject, while the *Fugue* finishes with a reminiscence of the *Prelude.*

Suite. New York: G. Schirmer, 1930. Dedicated to Isidor Philipp. *Allemande; Courante; Gavotte; Sarabande; Bourrée; Sicilienne; Menuet; Gigue.*

> The entire suite is unusually homogenous, notwithstanding the fact that each of the eight numbers is entirely different in character. . . . There is much detail, yet there is flow, a large line, a convincing polyphony, and a melodic and harmonic inevitableness; while the form is in rococo style, the contents are fresh and not conventional. [Letter from the composer to M. Aronson, Palma de Majorca, March 3, 1929; quoted in Nicholas, p. 137.]

At 37 pages, this is by far the longest solo work ever written for the left hand. D. NYPL.

Concert Album. New York: G. Schirmer, 1930; published separately in 1930 and 1931. Six compositions, later arranged for two hands by the composer.

Impromptu. Dedicated to Josef Lhevinne. One of Godowsky's more interesting works, especially in its rhythmic divisions.

Capriccio (Patetico). Dedicated to Ernest Hutcheson. An attempt at the "pathetic" style.

Intermezzo (Melanconico). Dedicated to Alexander Siloti. Fine opening.

Elegy. Dedicated to Gottfried Galston. Has a definite mood; not too difficult. In "Lewenthal."

Etude Macabre (originally called "Wailing Winds"). Dedicated to Emile Blanchet. An incredibly tricky perpetual motion meant to sound "murmuring and uncanny."

Meditation. Dedicated to Dimitri Tiompkin. Pleasant, not difficult. In "Lewenthal."

Symphonic Metamorphosis of the Schatz-Walzer Themes from "The Gypsy Baron" by Johann Strauss (1928). New York: G. Schirmer, 1941. Edited by Godowsky's son-in-law David Saperton, whose awesome technical equipment made him one of the few artists capable of mastering Godowsky's music. The piece was written for Paul Wittgenstein, though Godowsky wrote to his wife, "It is good music, very likely too good for Wittgenstein" (Vienna, May 6, 1928; quoted in Nicholas, p. 135). Even though Wittgenstein had exclusive use of it for three years, he never performed the *Metamorphosis,* and Godowsky eventually dedicated it to Simon Barere.

This was Godowsky's fourth paraphrase on the music of Johann Strauss, Jr., but his first for the left hand. A chain of appealing waltz tunes receives his typical harmonic coloring. The dance momentum is continuous, variety being achieved by seven tempo modifications. The finish is very exciting, although, surprisingly, Godowsky does not show off his ingenuity by combining two themes at once. A superbly written piece; playable after much practice.

Six Waltz Poems. New York: Carl Fischer, 1930. Dedicated to Carl Engel. Unlike in the preceding Strauss work, Godowsky is on his own here, and the tunes and harmonies are not especially affecting. But he shows himself to be a superb exponent of the sophisticated salon style. Cleverly written, not too hard. The first five are in moderate tempos, No. 6 is *con fuoco.*

Recordings

Paraphrases on Chopin's *Etudes:*
Geoffrey Douglas Madge: all 53 *Paraphrases* for one and two hands, Dante Studios, Paris. On four CDs: PSG8903–8906.
Marc-Andre Hamelin: op. 10, no 1; op. 25, no. 4; MV 1026.
Jorge Bolet: op. 10, no. 3; op. posth., no. 1; DSLO 26.
Shigeo Neriki: op. 10, nos. 3, 4, 8, 10, 11, and 12; SPF 1866.
Ian Hobson: op. 10, no. 12; Arabesque 6537.
Leopold Godowsky: op. 25 nos. 1 and 4, piano roll for Hupfeld (before 1922).

Original works:
Shura Cherkassky: *Waltz-Poem* No. 4; DSLO 7.
Marc-Andre Hamelin: *Prelude and Fugue;* MV 1026.
Jorge Bolet: *Elegie;* DSLO 417 361–1.

Antonio Gomezanda (b Lagos, Jalisco, 1894; d Mexico City, 1961). Pianist and composer.
Vieja danza: sobre un antiguo tema mexicano (for voice and piano or piano left-hand solo). Mexico: Ediciones del Instituto Musical "Gomezando." Indiana University.

J. Elise Gordon
The Left Hand Goes Into Training. London: Stainer & Bell, 1933. A dozen little two-liners for beginners, entitled "special games." L of C.

Alexandre Edouard Goria (b Paris, 1823; d Paris, 1860). Outstanding pianist, successful teacher, and writer of drawing-room pieces.
Sérénade et Variations finales, op. 9. Mainz: Schott, c. 1846. In Ruthardt/Peters Album. Not strictly for left hand alone: after the opening left-hand *Sérénade,* the right hand joins in for some showy variations. The tune is banal, with awkward breaks.

Danny Gould
Running Arpeggios. Brooklyn, 1947. A compendium of seventh chords in extended positions for jazz pianists. L of C.

Edouard Durand de Grau
Ange si pur: Romance de l'opera La Favorita de Donizetti, op. 11. Mainz: Schott, 1864. Brit. Lib.

C. Dieterich Graue
Kurze Melodische Stüdien, op. 25. Bremen: Schwers & Haake, c. 1888. Vol. I: *Präludium; Marsch; Elegie; Intermezzo.* Vol. II: *Nocturne; Idylle; Nachspiel.* Brit. Lib.

W. J. Greentree
Indian Legend, op. 77, no. 1; *Twilight Shadows,* op. 77, no. 2. A. Schmidt, 1919. Two very
simple works. L of C.

Carl William Greulich (1796–1837). Important Berlin piano pedagogue who may have
picked up the idea of left-hand music from his teacher Ludwig Berger. The original editions of the following pieces are not available, but the first two can be seen in Köhler's
op. 302, the third in "Lewenthal." Musically, Greulich cannot be called an important
composer, but the B minor *Study* is a *moto perpetuo* of technical value.
Chamber Study in E Major, op. 19.
Study in B minor, op. 19.
Velocity Study in F-sharp minor.

Elliot Griffis (1893–1967). American composer and teacher, settled in Los Angeles. He
wrote film scores and many songs.
Piece for the Left Hand (à la Chaconne). New York2 Schroeder & Gunther, 1923. Free
    variations on a simple C minor progression. M-D. 4 pp. American Music Center.
Happy Song. Hollywood: Robert Brown, 1959.

Cor De Groot (b Amsterdam, 1914). Principal professor of piano at the Conservatory
of the Hague. In 1959 he hurt his right hand.
Apparitions. Seven short connected pieces of modest difficulty. The layout is bare; the
    harmony, owing something to Bartók, is very simple. In *6 Piano Pieces for Left
    Hand by Dutch Composers,* Amsterdam: Donemus, 1963 (along with more impres-
    sive music subsequently created for De Groot by colleagues).
Apparitions No. 6. In *5 Piano Pieces for Left Hand by Dutch composers,* Amsterdam: Don-
    emus, 1964.

Eric Gross (b Vienna, 1926). Studied in London, now teaching at the University of
Sydney; author of many film and television scores.
3 Pieces for 5 Fingers or 1 Hand, op. 133. In "Australian." *Scherzino; Contemplation; Dis-
    cussion.* Impressive music. Without being overly complicated, it has enough
    dynamic and metric shifts to pose challenges for a bright young person (see
    Ex. 39).

EX. 39. Gross: *Scherzino* (Allan Music, 1984), mm. 1–9.

Cornelius Gurlitt (b Altona, 1820; d Altona, 1901). German organist and author of countless piano pieces.
Impromptu in A minor, op. 185, no. 4. Boston: A.P. Schmidt, 1892. Though not musically significant, this is a really fine finger study. L of C.
La Plainte: Etude, op. 123. London: Augener, 1902. Brit. Lib.

Alfred Matthew Hale
For the Left Hand Alone, op. 95. London: Goodwin & Tabb, 1952. Two pieces, in ms. Brit. Lib.

Frederich Hall
Prelude in F. Melbourne: Allan & Co., 1926. A Gavotte. M-D. 5 pp. L of C.

Julius Handrock (b Naumburg, 1830; d Halle, 1894). Many of his studies remained popular.
Schule der Geläufigkeit (School of Facility), Vol II. Leipzig: Kahnt, c. 1883.

Ronald Hanmer. English-born, in Australia since 1975; writes film music.
1. *Click Go the Shears.* 2. *Waltzing Matilda.* In "Australian." What might have been nice transcriptions for children are somewhat marred by very fast leaping grace notes in the bass.

Michael Hannan (b Newcastle, New South Wales, 1949). Australian; specializes in piano music.
Modal Melodies for Single Hands. In "Australian." Twelve tunes in single notes using the white keys—two for each of the modes between D and B. Very fine, with good phrasing and dynamics. Appealing for young children and "ear-stretching" in the manner of Bartók's *Mikrokosmos*.

G. Adolf Hardt
Capriccio. Cologne: P.J. Tonger, c. 1882.

Cuthbert Harris (b 1870)
Left Hand Studies: 5 Easy Studies (for left or right hand). London: Warren & Phillips, 1930. Titled music for children. 5 pp. Brit. Lib.

Shirley Harris, editor (b Queensland, 1941). Specializes in teaching piano to "students with learning and coordinating difficulties and physical handicaps." She edited the volume *Piano Music for One Hand by Australian Composers* (Melbourne: Allans Music, 1984). Fourteen authors contributed to this excellent volume of music for children. 45 pp. E. to M-D. Harris wrote the Preface and one piece:
Playmates. Unpretentious, useful technically, resembling the left-hand part of a Bach *Invention.*

Rudolf Hasert (1826–1877). Berlin pianist. According to Pauer's Dictionary, "for several years he was unable to play because of muscular pain."
Fantaisie de bravour sur l'air Casta diva de Bellini. Offenbach: André, c. 1855.

Frederic L. Hatch
Träumerei, by Schumann. T. Presser, 1920. A literal transcription, transposed to D-flat. Too many breaks. L of C.

Gustav Havemann
Meine Täglichen Stüdien für die linke Hand. Leipzig: Franz Jost, 1913. Several pages of slow thirds and scales.

William R. Hawkey. New Zealand musician and administrator.
1. *Playmates.* 2. *Colours.* In "Australian." Charming pieces.

O. L. Hayes
One Hand Waltz. Century.

Robert Helps (b Passaic, NJ, 1929). American pianist and composer whose music shows the influence of his teacher Roger Sessions.
Music for Left Hand. New York: Associated, 1976. Helps offers interesting observations on the challenge of writing piano music for different numbers of hands:

> *Music for Left Hand* was written specifically for me during a period of my life when I was having right arm difficulties. It has always rated high on my own little list of my own "favorites" of my compositions. Using as a norm one-piano 2-hand music, I would say that a composer writing for one-piano left-hand has to face the availability of too few notes—notes that also tend to be too close together; 4-hand one-piano music tends to have the availability of too many notes; and 2-piano 4-hands has a potential overuse of duplicate pitches with a resultant tendency towards "honky tonk" sound. It is truly interesting and challenging to try to avoid these sonic pitfalls.
>
> I think all composers who have written for one-piano left-hand consciously and/or unconsciously try to make it *not* sound like just one hand—for both musical and pianistic reasons. Needless to say this tends to make for high-level difficulties. Anyway, I would briefly characterize my 3 pieces as No. 1—highly textural and "impressionistic"; No. 2—vocal; No. 3—virtuosic—in this case, a toccata. [Letter to the author.]

These pieces make a strong statement; their craggy severity and atonal language may not be for every taste. Except for one rhythmic problem (3 against 4), the first two pieces are only moderately difficult, while the third is a veritable finger-twister, taking the player to the very top of the keyboard.

Oscar van Hemel (b Antwerp, 1892; d Hilversum, 1981).
Sonatina. In *5 Piano Pieces for Left Hand by Dutch Composers,* Amsterdam: Donemus, 1964.

Swan Hennessy (b Dublin, 1866; d Paris, 1929). An Irishman who lived most of his life in Paris.
2 Etudes. Paris: J. Hamelle, n.d. A few hard spots, musically poor.
Introduction, XII Variations et Fugue. Paris: E. Demets, 1910. From a strange volume of piano works, all based on "Chopsticks." The right hand has a version of this famous tune repeated *ad infinitum* and printed in small notes: should it be played? The left hand, printed in large notes, has a series of variations and a two-voice

fugue, vaguely related to "Chopsticks." Unfortunately, the musical results do not add up. 13 pp.

Marcella A. Henry
Gem from Flotow's Martha, 1913. *Shepherd's Lullaby,* 1911. *Annie Laurie,* 1915. *Robin Adair,* 1915. *Home, Sweet Home,* 1916. Philadelphia: Theodore Presser. Transcriptions. E. L of C.

Hans Werner Henze (b Gütersloh, Westphalia, 1926) German
La Mano sinistra: Piece for Leon. Mainz and New York: Schott, 1990. Written for Leon Fleisher. Rhapsodic, scored without barlines on three staves. Vivid, much tension through extreme dynamic contrasts; very complex rhythmic divisions. 8 pp. D. Chicago Public Library.

Paul-Silva Herard
Etude, op. 103, no. 12. From *12 Etudes pianistiques pour la main gauche.* Paris: Alphonse Leduc, 1910. The first eleven in this set are works for two hands emphasizing some left-hand technical problem, in the manner of Czerny. The twelfth is a fairly easy *Andantino* waltz for left hand alone. Each of the two-hand studies has a good preparatory left-hand exercise.

Marjorie Hicks (b London, 1905). Canadian organist, pianist, and composer.
2 Indispositions. Don Mills, Ontario: BMI Canada, Ltd., 1969. No. 1. *Indisposed Right Hand: Lamento.* Slow, wide-ranging triplets. Brooding and effective. 2 pp. M. (No. 2., *Indisposed Left Hand,* is for right hand alone.) Eastern Illinois University.

A.L. Hirst
Toujours prêt, op. 23, no. 5. London: Phillips & Page, 1913. Brit. Lib.

Neil Hobson
Seven Jazz Improvisations on Songs of the '30s, arranged for one hand. *Foggy Day; Georgia; Manhattan; Miss Otis Regrets; Skylark; The Folks Who live on the Hill; They can't take that away from me.* Available from Disabled Living Foundation.

Caesar Hochstetter
Album für einhändige Klavierspiel: 8 Stücke von Bach, Chopin, Schumann, Reger und Zichy (for left or right hand). Leipzig: Breitkopf & Härtel, c. 1915. Includes transcriptions.

Paul Höffer (b Barmen, 1895; d Berlin, 1949). Director of the Berlin Hochschule für Musik.
2 Etüden from *12 Etüden* (1942). In "Georgii." 1. *Largo:* solemn and funereal, reminiscent of Reger. 2. *Allegro vivace:* more difficult.

Richard Hoffman (b Manchester, 1831; d Mt. Kisco, NY, 1909). English-born pianist who studied with Liszt. He moved to New York and became a vital force in the city's musical life. His *Recollections* (New York: Scribner's, 1910) contains colorful first-hand descriptions of Thalberg, Liszt, Gottschalk, and many others.
Venetian Serenade. Theodore Presser, 1907. Quite easy, a fair imitation of Italian popular song style. L of C.

Josef Casimir Hofmann (b Krakow, 1876; d Los Angeles, 1957). This fabled Polish-born pianist was the only student of Anton Rubinstein. The first pianist ever to record (an 1887 cylinder), he published over one hundred works under the pseudonym Michael Dvorsky. Hofmann also held more than seventy copyrights for scientific and mechanical inventions.

Etude in C major, op. 32. Leipzig: C. Dieckmann; New York: E. Schubert & Co., n.d. Published under his own name, and one of the best left-hand pieces in salon style from the turn-of-the-century. A somewhat "schmaltzy" opening (Ex.40) leads into a *marziale*. A fine piano roll performance by Hofmann exists on LP: Everet X918.

EX. 40. Hofmann: *Etude* (C. Dieckmann, n.d. [c. 1905?]), mm. 1–7.

Alexis Hollaender (b Silesia, 1840; d Berlin, 1924). A major figure in Berlin's musical life, as both pianist and conductor. He introduced the public there to Brahms's *German Requiem* and played the first Berlin performances of several major Schumann piano works, including *Kreisleriana* and the *Symphonic Etudes*. Hollaender was also important as an editor of Schumann's piano music. After Paul Wittgenstein lost his right arm in World War I, he spent much time in libraries looking for left-hand music to play, and Hollaender was among the few composers who pleased him. Among late nineteenth- and early twentieth-century music, his works stand out dramatically from the others. Hollaender combined a superior melodic gift with extremely sound harmonic progressions. He used the left hand well, and never fell into two-hand thinking (awkward breaks, etc.).

6 Klavierstücke, op. 31. Berlin: Schlesinger, 1884. 1. *Abendlied*. 2. *Etude*. 3. *Melodie*. These two charming pages could almost have been written by Schumann (see Ex.41). 4. *Walzer*. 5. *Perpetuum mobile*. Highly recommended as an etude, 5 pp. 6. *Jaglied*. L of C.

6 Klavierstücke, op. 52. Berlin: Schlesinger, 1897. *Lied; Scherzino; Studie; Menuetto; Romanze; Canon*. L of C.

6 Fantasiestücke, op. 66. Berlin: Schlesinger, c. 1916. *Gavotte; Pilgerzug; Nachtlicher Ritt; Schlummerlied; Das Bächlein; Ländler*.

EX. 41. Hollaender: *Melodie* (M. Schlesinger, 1884), mm. 1–9.

Camillo Horn (b Bohemia, 1860; d Vienna, 1941). Studied with Bruckner in Vienna and settled there; a choral conductor and music critic.
Albumblatt, op. 33, no. 1. Leipzig: C.F. Kahnt, 1908. *Langsam,* loose in form and sentimental. M-D. L of C.
Fantasie, op. 33, no. 2.

Christina Hovemann
Twilight Shadows. Harold Flammer, 1946. Simple teaching piece. NYPL.

Hans Huber (b Eppenburg, Solothurn, 1852; d Locarno, 1921). According to Grove's Dictionary, Huber "can perhaps be regarded as the most important Swiss composer of the 19th century." He was active as a piano teacher.
Die Schulung der linken Hand includes a set of exercises for the left hand alone.

Charles Huerter. Born in Brooklyn, organist and composer of religious music based in Syracuse, NY.
Six Compositions. Boston: B.F. Wood, 1926. *Spring's Magic; The White Butterfly; From the Southland; Restless Moments; Summer Moon; Bridlepaths.* L of C.
Dancing in the Sunlight. G. Schirmer, 1927.
Mask Dance; Tango. G. Schirmer, 1927.
Marching. G. Schirmer, 1927.
By the Firelight. G. Schirmer, 1928.
Huerter's eleven short pieces are in that sentimental vein so prevalent in turn-of-the-century American piano music. As often happens, the quicker pieces are best, in this case *Tango* and *Dancing in the Sunlight.* NYPL.

Ferdinand Hummel (b Berlin, 1855; d Berlin, 1928). A performing harpist and composer of operas, no relation to Johann Nepomuk Hummel, the famous rival of Beethoven.
5 Klavierstücke, op. 43. Leipzig: C.F.W. Siegel. *Frühlingsgrass; Etude; Walzer; Lied; Marsch.* The repetitiveness combined with a distinct lack of imagination make one ponder the experience of sitting through an opera by Hummel. Grateful scoring; the *Etude* is a good work-out. Nos. 1, 2, and 3 at Boston University, Nos. 4 and 5 at NYPL.

Miriam Hyde (b Adelaide, South Australia, 1913). She studied in London and recorded her own *Concerto*. Her *3 Studies* for the right hand alone were the result of a 1982 accident in which her left arm was broken.

Susan Bray's Album, a set of pieces for left hand, owes its existence to a touching personal encounter Hyde had on a concert tour of New South Wales in the 1940s. She was playing some piano music at the home of a friend, and among the works was her own *Intermezzo* for the left hand alone:

> At the conclusion of the Intermezzo, a Mr. Ken Bray seemed quite moved, and said that he had no idea that one hand could produce music that sounded so complete and satisfying. His third, and youngest daughter, Susan had been born without a right hand. He and his wife, Esme, realized that perhaps Susan could do some piano study after all. I was moved, too, and at once started writing some elementary pieces for left hand, in further train journeys and in my hotels, at night.

The *Album,* reprinted in "Australian," contains ten pieces in as many pages, simple and quite charming. Moving mostly one note at a time in uncomplicated patterns, each has a simple poem along with the title. Perfect for very young children.
Intermezzo, op. 6.

J.A. Ide, editor
Ballade for Piano. Baltimore: George Willig & Co., 1884. Somewhat unfocused musically. D. L of C.

Daniel Jones
"Evening Star," from Wagner's *Tannhäuser.* St. Louis: Shattinger Music Co., 1920. Lengthy—it includes the entire introduction—and very faithful harmonically, except for a lapse in the last two lines. Requires good tremolos. L of C.

Rafael Joseffy (b Hunfalu, 1852; d New York City, 1915). Hungarian pianist who finished his studies with Liszt in Weimar. He debuted in America in 1879, settled there, and published a *School of Advanced Piano Playing* (1902).
Gavotte from J.S. Bach's *Partita* No. 3 for violin in E major. E. Schuberth, 1880. In "Lewenthal." A fairly straightforward transcription of Bach's original, predominantly in single notes. Joseffy fills out some chords; he also invents basses, not all of which arise inevitably out of the original. The ornaments are awkwardly realized and can be changed. A good M-D piece for students.

Alfred de Kaiser (b Brussels, 1872; d Bournemouth, 1917). Settled in England, de-Germanicizing his name to De Keyser during World War I.
Ballade. In *Melodious Studies,* edited by R. H. Bellairs. London: Enoch & Sons, 1905. Brit. Lib.

Friederich Kalkbrenner (b en route from Kassel to Berlin, 1785; d Enghien-les Bains, 1849). French, of German extraction. As one of the first performers to make an international career, he was probably the world's most famous pianist between 1825 and 1835. Much sought-after as a teacher (he almost convinced Chopin to study with him), Kalkbrenner had a lucrative share in Pleyel's piano business. Kalkbrenner's *Sonata,* written for two hands with a difficult left-hand part, is sometimes mistakenly listed as a work for left hand alone.

Fugue in G (n.d.). In "Lewenthal." The first one-handed fugue and one of the more modest. Counterpoint is at a minimum, with the four voices resting continually. It has a certain lilt and, with the exception of a few octaves, no difficulties. 2 pp.

Maurice Karkoff (b Stockholm, 1927). His educational music for piano and chorus is highly regarded in Sweden.

3 Klavierstücke, op. 46 (1959). Unpublished ms. 1. *Impromptu;* 2. *Intermezzo Capriccioso;* 3. *Elegie.* Written for the Dutch pianist Cor de Groot, who had suffered an injury to his right hand. Isolated notes, extremely bare and simple; atonal. 6 min. Available from Swedish Music Information Center, Box 27 327, S-102 54 Stockholm.

Erich Kauffman-Jassoy (b Wiesbaden, 1877). A student of Grieg.

Anschlagstudie. Dresden: J. Gunther, c. 1921.

Don Kay (b Smithton, Tasmania, 1933). Teacher at the University of Tasmania. He has written much theater and puppet music.

For Shirley Harris. In "Australian." Two really fine pieces at a child's level—an introduction to the art of using the hand for simultaneous tasks and a study in dynamic gradations.

Joseph Christoph Kessler (b Augsburg, 1800; d Vienna, 1872). German pianist to whom Chopin dedicated his *24 Preludes.* According to Pauer's *Dictionary of Pianists,* Liszt strongly praised Kessler's *Studies,* op. 21 and op. 51.

Etude in F minor. In Louis Köhler's *School for the Left Hand,* op. 302. Recommended.

Otto Klauwell (b Langensalza, 1851; d Cologne, 1917). German composer and writer on music. A pupil of Reinecke, he taught at the Cologne Conservatory.

3 Klavierstücke, op. 34. Trier: Vom Ende.

Fritz Kley

Gem from Flotow's Martha. Washington, D.C.: John F. Ellis, 1896. Awkward, needs two hands for a proper performance. L of C.

Ernst-Lothar v. Knorr (b Eitorf, 1896) German

1. *Serenade:* somber, modest demands. 2. *Etüde:* jagged perpetual motion. In "Georgii." M-D.

A. Knoth

"Ah! I Have Sighed to Rest Me," from Verdi's *Il Trovatore.* New York: A. Buchbaum, 1913. "Ah, che la morte ognora," the tenor solo from Act IV, Scene 1, in a harmonic and rhythmic travesty. L of C.

Erland Koch (b 1910). Swedish composition teacher, studied piano with Claudio Arrau. Professor of Harmony at Musikhögskolan in Stockholm.

Nocturnal Etude (1973) for left hand or (with added notes in parentheses) both hands. Stockholm: Gehrmanns Musikförlag, 1983. Dedicated to Esther Bodin. 6 pp. M. Available from Swedish Music Information Center, Box 27 327, S 102–54, Stockholm.

John Koehler
Melody. New York: G. Schirmer, 1908. A theme with two variations. 6 pp. M-D. L of C.

Albert C. Koeppler
"Romance" from Wagner's *Tannhäuser.* Chicago: A.C. Koeppler, 1911. A transcription of the "Song to the Evening Star," with unnecessary harmonic alterations; rather difficult, octaves. L of C.

Louis Köhler (b. Brunswick, 1820; d Königsberg, 1886.) According to *Baker's Biographical Dictionary of Musicians*, Köhler is "remembered exclusively for his albums of piano studies, which have been adopted in music schools all over the world; next to Czerny, he is the most popular purveyor of didactic piano literature."
Schule der linken Hand, op. 302. Leipzig: C.F. Peters, 1881. Consists largely of works for *two* hands by Czerny, Cramer, Bertini, Clementi, Kalkbrenner, and many others. Among the one-hand material are Köhler's simple transcriptions from opera and folk song, a group of exercises and scales, and etudes by Greulich, Kessler, and Berger. Arranged in order of progressive difficulty.
Wellen-Melodie: Etude, op. 86. c. 1865.

Ellis B. Kohs (b Chicago, 1916)
Ten Two-Voice Inventions, unpublished ms. (n.d.). Nos. 2 and 9 for left hand (nos. 3 and 8 for right hand). As described by Kohs, "they call for harmonics aided and abetted by the other hand which presses keys silently, which some may regard as 'cheating'." Available from American Composers Alliance, 170 W. 74 St., New York, NY 10023.

Klimenty Korchmarev (b 1899; d Moscow, 1958). Winner of the Stalin Prize for many revolutionary works of "social significance."
Prelude. Moscow, 1922. Beautifully written in the Russian Romantic style, à la Scriabin (see Ex.42). M. L of C.

EX. 42. **Korchmarev:** *Prelude* (Moscow: n.p., 1922), mm. 1–4.

Eduard Krause (1837–1892).
Schule der linken Hand, op. 80: *40 Übungen und Etüden für höhere und höchste Ausbildung.* Hug.
10 Etüden, op. 15.

Richard Krentzlin (1864–1956). German piano pedagogue.
3 Pieces. Philadelphia: Theodore Presser, 1925. *Romance; Voices at Evening; Festival Polonaise.* Salon music. M-D. L of C.

C.W. Krogman (b 1860; d Boston, 1943). Bostonian teacher who published hundreds of piano pieces.
3 Morceaux, op. 90. Boston: B.F. Wood, 1911. *Valse Viennoise; Marche Héroïque; Poème d'Amour.* L of C.
Two Waltz Episodes, op. 81. Boston: Oliver Ditson, 1912. *L'Ingénue; La Coquette.*
Berceuse, op. 99, no. 2.
Modest in scope, in a dated musical style. L of C.

Hans Kulla
Variations über "Verstohlen geht der Mond auf." In "Georgii." This fine old German minstrel tune is the same one Brahms used for the variations forming the slow movement of his *Sonata* in C, op. 1. But Kulla's four free variations are no match for the master. There is a place "to improvise" before the end and some good canonic writing. M.

Rudolf Kündinger (b 1832). Bavarian.
14 Klavierübungen. Leipzig: Rahter, c. 1890.

Elizabeth Kunger
Mélodie. E. Schubert & Co., 1926. Antiquated style, simple. L of C.

Charles Kunkel (b Sipperfeld, Rheinfalz, 1840; d St. Louis, 1923). In America from 1848, founder of the St. Louis Conservatory and a shining light in the German-American musical community. He established music publishing in St. Louis, and his piano "method" was praised by Liszt.
Grand Concert Pieces. (n.p., n.d.) Except for No. 5, all are transcriptions. 1. *Sextet* from Donizetti's *Lucia di Lammermoor,* a copy of Liszt's two-hand paraphrase—including his introduction—without an acknowledgment to Liszt! D. 2. *Quartet* from Verdi's *Rigoletto.* 3. *Miserere* from Verdi's *Il Trovatore,* the entire scene, recitatives and all; some rhythmic falsifications. 4. *Home, Sweet Home.* 5. *The Banjo,* a clever imitation of this instrument in the spirit of Gottschalk; long and effective; recommended; D. 6. *Old Black Joe;* long (12 pp.); D. 7. *Old Folks at Home.*

Walter Lang (b Basel, 1896; d Baden, canton of Aargau, 1966). Swiss pianist with close ties to the Jaques-Dalcroze Institute and founder of the Lang Trio.
Sonata (Sonatine) in E minor, op. 4. Ries & Erler, 1918. Curtis Institute.
10 Klavier-Etüden, op. 74. Hug, 1974. No. 5 is for left hand alone. Two voices. M-D.

T. Langlois (b 1909).
A une main. New York: Associated.

Joan Last (b Sussex, 1908). British, professor of piano at the Royal Academy and prolific composer.
Introduction to the Suite. Bosworth.

Rhythmic Reading. Bosworth.
Right Hand, Left Hand. Freeman.

Gustav Lazarus (b Cologne, 1861; d Berlin, 1920). German pianist who scored a European success, important as a teacher in Berlin.
Etude, op. 19, no. 5. Leipzig: Dietrich, c. 1888.

Jeffrey Leask (b Melbourne, 1944). Music educator and composer in Melbourne.
Fifths and Thirds. In "Australian." Pleasant children's music in a naive style.

Luise Adolpha Le Beau (b Rastatt, 1850; d Baden-Baden, 1927). German student of Clara Schumann. Highly regarded by Hanslick, she performed her own music in many cities.
Improvisata: Etude, op. 30. Hamburg: Crainz, c. 1883.

Ton De Leeuw (b Rotterdam, 1926). Dutch composer with a strong interest in non-European compositional systems; Director of the Amsterdam Conservatory.
Linkenhand en Rechterhand. Amsterdam: Donemus, 1976. Photo of ms. Very primitive, moving slowly note by note. 2 pp. NYPL.
Cinq Etudes. Amsterdam: Donemus, 1951. Maurice Hinson calls it "his most successful works for piano." No. 3 is for left hand. M-D.

Theodor Leschetizky [Teodor Leszetycki] (b Lancut, Galicia, 1830; d Dresden, 1915). Studied with Czerny, whose methods he continued. Also close to Anton Rubinstein, for whom he headed the Piano Department at the St. Petersburg Conservatory. Leschetizky was extraordinarily successful as a teacher in Vienna. He was also active as a conductor, and all pianists will enjoy his memorable judgment: "It is harder to play six bars well on the piano than to conduct the whole of Beethoven's Ninth Symphony."
Andante Finale from *Lucia di Lammermoor,* op. 13. Berlin: Schlesinger, n.d. Dedicated to Alexander Dreyschock. Reprinted, New York: G. Schirmer, 1906; Philadelphia: Hatch Music Co., 1909 (transposed from D-flat to C). The title is a misnomer, for this is the famous *Sextet* from Donizetti's opera. Very difficult, with fistfuls of chords and arpeggios, so easy to miss on the many black keys of D-flat major. Leschetizky added his own long, irrelevant preamble (compare this to Liszt's two-hand transcription of the same music, with his organic and significant introduction). Of course, any arrangement of the *Lucia Sextet* has the advantage of two stirring melodies, but here the over-all artistic effect is of a difficult, slightly lumbering stunt. Judging by the number of reprints, this thorny arrangement was one of the most popular of all creations for the left hand.

Raymond Lewenthal, editor (b San Antonio, 1926; d Hudson, NY, 1988). Pianist, one of the great specialists in unusual Romantic repertoire.
Piano Music for One Hand. New York: G. Schirmer, 1972. A well-chosen anthology of 30 works by Bartók, Reger, Saint-Saëns, Godowsky, and Moskowski, among others. The emphasis is on moderate difficulty: Godowsky is represented by two of his easiest pieces. The Preface offers advice on playing and pedaling left hand music. There is also a brief, colorfully written history of the literature, though Lewenthal mistakenly attributes pioneering left-hand music to the nineteenth-century Italian pianists Döhler and Pollini.

Heinrich Lichner (1829–1898)

3 Romanzen, op. 267. Leipzig: Siegel, 1886. No. 2: fairly easy "parlor music," limited.
   No. 2 at NYPL.

Dinu Lipatti (b Bucharest, 1917; d Geneva, 1950). Studied piano with Musicescu and
Cortot, and composition with Dukas and Boulanger.

Sonatina. Paris: Editions Salabert, 1953. Lipatti wrote in a dry, neo-classical style—clarity was one of his great strengths as a pianist. Plain textures, together with musical
   ideas not quite interesting enough to sustain entire movements. Of the three movements, the finale is best.

Franz Liszt (b Raiding, near Sopron 1811; d Bayreuth, 1886)

Ungarns Gott (Hungary's God) (1881). In New Edition of the Complete Works, vol. xvii,
   Kassel and Budapest, 1970; also in "Lewenthal." A transcription of the next-to-last
   of Liszt's many songs, arranged for his student and friend, the one-armed pianist
   Count Geza Zichy (see p. 29). Sectional and improvisational in feeling, it has the
   stark simplicity and strange harmonic shifts typical of Liszt's late piano music. M.

Although he wrote no extended works for one hand, Liszt more than once gave short
solos to the left hand, as in the first (and practically unknown) version of his *Sonetto
del Petrarca* 104 (see Ex.43).

EX. 43. **Liszt:** *Sonetto del Petrarca 104* **(Breitkopf & Härtel, complete
works, 1907–1936; reprint, Gregg Press, 1966), mm. 20–29.**

Hans Lorenzen

Klaviermusik für Einhander allein und mit Partner (3 books). Stiftung Rehabilitation Heidelberg.

Alain Louvier (b Paris, 1945). Student of Messiaen; head of the National Conservatory
of Music in Paris.

Etude pour agresseurs (Etude no. 37). Paris: Alphonse Leduc, 1973. Written for French
   pianist Lelia Gousseau. One of the most *avant garde* works for one hand.

> *Etudes pour agresseurs* is the general term for a personal technique which seeks to
> accustom the interpreter to means of attacking the keyboard: fingers, palms, wrists,
> forearms, which are the object of a very precise sonorous and gestural search. . . . This
> great cycle seeks a greater sonorous plenitude for the instrument, and not gratuitous
> violence. [Publisher's catalogue.]

A chart of instructions details the striking, smashing, and sliding techniques. There is some improvisation, and in places the pitches are left to the performer's discretion (see Ex.44). Once the extremely detailed instructions are deciphered there are no technical difficulties in the traditional sense. 11 min.

EX. 44. Louvier: *Etude pour agresseurs* (Alphonse Leduc, 1973), mm. 1–2.

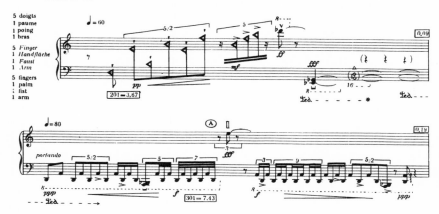

Joan Lovell

6 Pieces: The Circus. London: Augener, Ltd., 1957. Worthy short pieces for beginners, with circus-related titles. L of C.

Ernst Ludwig. Professor of Piano at the Vienna Academy.
24 Studien. Vienna: Doblinger (n.d.).

Litta Lynn

A Night Song, op. 10. Boston: B.F. Wood, 1913. Dated salon-style music. M-E. L of C.

Hamilton C. Macdougall

Graded Material for the Left Hand, Grades II to IV. Boston: Oliver Ditson Co., 1918. Contains two-hand music, as well as pieces for left hand alone by Gurlitt (6 studies), Albert Biehl, Stephen Heller (arranged), and Ernest Pauer (a good double-note etude). Other works by Hollaender, Spindler, Hummel, and Preyer.

Alexander Macfadyen (b Milwaukee, 1879; d Milwaukee, 1936).
Believe Me, If All Those Endearing Young Charms. Chicago: Badger Music Publishing Co., 1929. Transcription. M-E. L of C, Brit. Lib.

Wilhelm Maler (b Heidelberg, 1902; d Hamburg, 1976). Director of the Detmold Academy and prominent composition teacher.
Präludium und Fuge. In "Georgii." Written for Lothar Quast. *Prelude* is *tranquillo; Fugue* has nice counterpoint. Tonally conservative. An alternate fingering is given for right-handed performers.

Charles Malherbe (b Paris, 1853; d Cormeilles, Eure, 1911). French musicologist and owner of an immense collection of autograph scores; editor of the works of Rameau and Berlioz.

Petite Etude. Paris: Durand et fils, n.d. Malherbe's piece shares one quality with his beloved Berlioz—a certain harmonic illogicality—without possessing any of his virtues. University of Chicago.

Aldo Mantia (1903–1982). Italian, taught in Rome.

Profond Sommeil (c. 1937). A transcription of Rossini's piano piece, No. 7 of Book 7 (*Album de Chaumières*) from his *Péchés de Vieillesse* (Sins of Old Age). A lovely melancholy tune in B minor, *mesto*, in an unusual scoring—the melody is set below the accompaniment. L of C.

Eric Mareo

Two Studies: Lament and Allegretto. London: Elkin Co., 1924. Good for a young person. E. NYPL.

Two Bagatelles. London: Stainer & Bell, 1926. L of C.

Two Diversions. London: Augener, 1925. Very much like popular songs. M. L of C.

Wladyslawa Markiewiczowna (b 1900). Polish

Zniwiarze Etiuda Na Lewa Reke (Reaper's Etude for Left Hand), No. 4. Kolobowe Obrazki, Zabrze: Dom Muzyki Polskiej. Gavotte type in A major. E. (No. 5 is for right hand.) 1 p. NYPL.

R. Ch. Martin

Ecole de la main gauche, moyenne force, op. 89 and op. 92. Paris: Alphonse Leduc, 1920. 16 pieces of medium difficulty, mostly original works, plus a few transcriptions. Idiomatically laid out, though musically flat. L of C.

Eduard Marxsen (b Nienstadten, near Altona, 1806; d Altona, 1887). A sought-after teacher in Hamburg, remembered today for his student, the young Johannes Brahms. Although Brahms later claimed he learned nothing from him, Marxsen drilled him in counterpoint and certainly encouraged his interest in past musical eras.

Hommage à Dreyschock: 3 Impromptus, op. 33. Before 1844. No. 2, *La Ricordanza,* is in "Lewenthal." A tribute to the great left-hand player Dreyschock, this early work is only of historical interest.

Exercices en 6 pièces caracteristiques, op. 40. c. 1844.

Janez Matičič (b 1926). Yugoslavian, student of Skerjanc and Boulanger.

Tri Etude, 1954. Yugoslavia.

Tri Etude, 1961. Yugo: Drustvo Slovenskih Skladateljev, 1961.

In his ambitious studies, written in a late-Romantic style, Matičič manages to weave several melodic threads at once. L of C.

E. Maurat

Prelude, op. 4, no. 9, from *Le premier livre des preludes.* Paris: Eschig, 1951. Bears the inscription: "Le feu le plus ardent est celui qui se consume le plus vite—Pindare. À la mémoire d'André Gédalge." Fine chromatic late-Romantic feeling, but produces a fragmentary effect when played alone—it would be best grouped with some of the other *Preludes*. 2 pp.

George Pratt Maxim
Old Black Joe by Stephen Foster. Boston Music Co., 1939. A transcription; rather sophisticated polyphony, subtler than many left-hand arrangements. L of C.

Frederich Maxson (b New Jersey, 1862; d Philadelphia, 1934). American organist who studied in Paris, active in Philadelphia.
Reverie. Philadelphia: F.A. North, 1888. M. L of C.

Alfonso Melendez (b 1930)
Arpegio in A-flat minor, op. 15, no. 2. Casa Amarella. 2 pp. Indiana University.

W.P. Mero
Believe Me, If All Those Endearing Young Charms. T. Presser, 1915. Transcription. Very simple strummed chords. L of C.

Paul Mertz
Rhythmic Etude. Ms. (1934). Written in "swing" style. L of C.

Hans Mettke
Sweet Sixteen. Cincinnati: John Church, 1893. A rather mawkish tune. E. L of C.

Marcel Mihalovici (b Bucharest, 1898; d c. 1987). French composer of Rumanian origin, married to French pianist Monique Haas.
Passacaille, op. 105 (1975). Paris: Salabert, 1982. Written for the French pianist Lelia Gousseau. A major contemporary work, an immense structure built on a ground bass of eight measures. Its eighteen repetitions develop this melody with ever-increasing freedom. The ground is transposed, placed in the soprano, used as a canon against itself. The rhythm is transformed, various countermelodies enter, etc. Each variation (as he calls them) has its own tempo and character. Contemporary notation is employed; contains clusters, glissandi, and atonal harmony. The one weakness is a kind of two-hand thinking: for a proper rendering the left hand continually needs to be in two places at once. This means constant resort to the pedal for sustaining voices, but in a texture already bristling with dissonances and dense sound, the result is often confusion. 16 min. D.

Enrico Mineo
Autumn Leaves (Foglie d'autunno). Boston: Oliver Ditson, 1928. Dedicated to Graziella Consoli. Salon waltz. M.

Alfonso Montecino (b Osorno, 1924). Chilean; studied composition with Sessions at Juilliard and piano with Arrau.
Composición en 3 movimentos (1951). Ms. 11 pp. Indiana University.

Xavier Montsalvatge (b Gerona, 1912). Spanish composer and critic.
Si, a Mompou. Madrid: Union Musical Española, 1985. *Calmato,* atonal. M-D. L of C.

Robert A. Morrow
Concert Study. New York: Breitkopf & Härtel. Thorny technical problems. L of C.

Moritz Moszkowski (b Breslau, 1854; d Paris, 1925). German pianist of Polish descent. He studied with Kullak in Berlin, taught at his Conservatory for many years, and spent the last decades of his life in Paris. Such works as *Etincelles, Rhapsodie Espagnole* (he was a kind of Spanish specialist), and the *Concerto* in E had an extraordinary vogue, so it is distressing to learn that Moszkowski ended his life in poverty.

12 Etudes, op. 92. Paris: Enoch & Cie., 1915. These are far less known than the much-practiced etudes for two hands, op. 72. Moszkowski knew well how to codify a particular technical problem, and those seeking the perfect studies for one hand need go no further. Many modestly equipped students clumsily practicing Chopin's *"Revolutionary"* Etude would gain a lot from the G minor *Study* (see Ex.3, p. 9). The *Etude* in A minor is a little easier (see Ex.45). There are double notes (Ex.46) and a good octave study. Moszkowski's harmonic progressions are extremely sound, there is integrity to his music, and at its best it conjures up a mood of great affection (Ex.47). This may be salon music, but no one ever did it better.

EX. 45. Moszkowski: *Etude* no. 2 (Enoch & Cie., 1915), mm. 1–3.

EX. 46. Moszkowski: *Etude* no. 3 (Enoch & Cie., 1915), mm. 1–2.

EX. 47. Moszkowski: *Etude* no. 11 (Enoch & Cie., 1915), mm. 1–6.

Carl Moter
Romanze. Theodore Presser, 1917. Light-weight. L of C.

Christine A. Murow
Sounds for One Hand: Five Lyric Studies. Willis Music, 1986.

Maryanne Nagy
One-Handed Solitaire. New York: Lee Roberts, 1970.

Alberto Nepomuceno (b Fortaleza, 1864; d Rio de Janeiro, 1920). Composer and conductor who played a major role in the emergence of musical nationalism in Brazil.
Nocturne. New York: G. Schirmer, 1917. Conservative Romantic music of a superior sort.

Newstead
Pieces For Left Hand Alone, op. 63. B.F. Wood. *Dream Hours; Sunlit Joys; In the Fading Sunset; Plantation Dance; Sea Flowers; Wayside Gardens.*

Rudolf Niemann (b Holstein, 1838; d Wiesbaden, 1898). Student of Moscheles and Bülow; taught at Wiesbaden.
3 Kleine Konzertstücke, op. 40. Leipzig: Fr. Kistner, 1896. Dedicated to Geza Zichy. *Romanze; Alla Gavotte; Presto (Perpetuum mobile).* 6 pp. D. *Presto* at L of C.

Isabel Stewart North
The Fable. Bradford, Pa.: North Publishing Co., 1912. A multisectioned "melodrama" illustrating the fairy tale printed on the first page.

Old Time Music Hall Songs, 1987. 14 pp. Available from Disabled Living Foundation.

Lynn Freeman Olson
Marine's Hymn; Greensleeves; She Wore a Yellow Ribbon; Serenade; Londonderry Air; Entr'acte. In the Carl Fischer catalogue, listing piano compositions on the 1991–1994 Junior Festivals List, National Federation of Music Clubs: Piano One Hand at 6 graded levels of difficulty.

Julia O'Neill
Musing. London: B.F. Wood Music Co., 1932. Sentimental "parlor" music. L of C.

Preston Ware Orem (1865–1938). American author of a widely used *Harmony Book for Beginners.*
Sextet from Lucia di Lammermoor. T. Presser, 1919. Transcription (in C major) of the famed ensemble from Donizetti's opera, with some harmonic alterations. L of C.

Léon Orthel (b Roosendaal, North Brabant, 1905). Dutch professor at the conservatories of the Hague (piano) and Amsterdam (composition).
Sonatina No. 5 (1959). In *6 Pieces for Left Hand by Dutch Composers,* Amsterdam: Donemus, 1963. A three-movement work in a dry, almost primitive style of writing. M.

Hans Osieck (b Amsterdam, 1910)
Tema con Variazioni. In *5 Pieces for Left Hand by Dutch Composers,* Amsterdam: Donemus, 1964.

Wouter Paap (b Utrecht, 1908). Self-taught Dutch composer and author of many
books.
Danse Gauche. In *5 Pieces for Left Hand by Dutch Composers,* Donemus, 1964.

Arthur Ross Parsons (b Ohio, 1847; d Mt. Kisco, NY, 1933). After studies in Germany
with Moscheles and Tausig, he settled in New York City, where he became the "dean"'
of piano teachers.
Solfeggietto by C.P.E. Bach. New York: G. Schirmer, 1885. In "Lewenthal." A transcription of the most famous of Bach's 3 *Solfeggii.* By faithful adherence to the original
it becomes quite tricky in a few spots. A worthwhile study.

Ernst Pauer (1826–1905). Austrian who spent many years in London. He taught at the
Royal Academy and gave a series of historical chronological recitals. Pauer prepared
editions of older keyboard music and arranged much repertoire for two, four, and eight
hands.
The Culture of the Left Hand. London: Augener, 1907. Books I, II, and IV are for left
hand alone; Book III is "for two hands, with special regard for the left hand."
12 Etudes caracteristiques pour la main gauche seule. London: Augener, 1892.
Suite pour la main gauche. London: Augener, 1890.
All in Brit. Lib.

Herman Perlet (1864–1916)
Dance Grace, op. 15, no. 3. New York: Witmark & Sons, 1911. Brit. Lib.

Pierre Perny (b 1824)
Surprise: Mélodie, op. 78.
Quartet [Sextet] *from Lucia di Lammermoor,* op. 81. Milan: Ricordi, c. 1848.

Darrell Peter (b Pawnee, Oklahoma, 1918). Active in New York City.
Prelude in E minor. St. Louis: Art Publishing Society, 1960. A simple sarabande, tonal.

Felix Petyrek (b Brno, 1892; d Vienna, 1951). Austrian, active in many cities, settled in
Vienna.
2 Tanzstücke. No. 2 is for left hand (No. 1 for right hand). In "Georgii." Fairly easy waltz
in B major, capturing a nice mood in a rather strange harmonic language.

Isidor Philipp (b Budapest, 1863; d Paris, 1958). French pianist and teacher of Hungarian origin. He studied at the Paris Conservatory, where he taught with extraordinary
success from 1893 to 1934. From World War II on he was in the United States and gave
a remarkable farewell performance at the age of 92. His many technical works are still
highly regarded.
Exercices et etudes techniques. Paris: Durand et fils, 1895. This volume—completely for
the left hand alone—opens with two dozen fine exercises. The main body of the

collection features an unusual type of "etude"—not music as such, but practice material. In other contexts Phillip was a composer, but his idea in this case (Georges Mathias, the author of the Preface, claims it to be a new idea) was to take a very large amount of music originally written for the right hand and transfer it to the left, simply leaving out the accompaniments (see Ex.48). Although Philipp drew on Chopin, Weber, Czerny, and Mendelssohn, one should not look here for aesthetic satisfaction, but for first-class digital drills. 41 pp.

EX. 48. **Schumann/Philipp:** *Toccata* (**Durand et fils, 1895), mm. 1–4.**

2 Etudes d'après Mendelssohn et Paganini. Paris: Alphonse Leduc, 1910. Transcriptions. No. 1 is Mendelssohn's op. 119 for piano, *Perpetuum mobile, prestissimo,* terrific; 5 pp. No. 2 is a *Moto Perpetuo* by Paganini; very useful. No. 1 has been reprinted, New York: G. Schirmer, 1931. L of C.

4 Etudes d'après Bach. Paris: E. Froment, 1903. Dedicated to Moriz Rosenthal. Transcriptions from Bach's *Sonatas* and *Partitas* for solo violin. 1. *Prelude* in E major; 2. *Bourrée* in B minor; 3. *Presto* in G minor; 4. *Chaconne* in D minor—far more difficult than Brahms's arrangement of the same work. Nos. 1 and 2, M-D; Nos. 3 and 4, D. All excellent studies. L of C.

Eduard Pirkhert (b Styria, 1817; d Vienna, 1881). A student of Czerny who taught at the Vienna Conservatory.

Thème: Etude in D-flat. No. 5 from *12 Etudes de salon,* op. 10. Paris: Mechetti, c. 1844. Vocal in feeling, fairly easy, chords in wide extensions. NYPL.

John Robert Poe. American teacher active in Columbus, Georgia.

Look Ma, One Hand: Pieces For One Hand Alone. San Diego, Cal.: Kjos West, 1990. Dedicated "To Jessica, who smashed her thumb." 13 very simple pieces for children, some for left hand, some for right; similar to nursery rhymes. Recommended.

V. Pohl (b Kiev, 1880).

Two Pieces, op. 19. Paris: M.P. Belaieff, 1947. 1. *Valse Impromptu;* 2. C major. Exceptionally well written in terms of texture and finger pattern: Pohl must have known Godowsky's works. An evocation of turn-of-the-century Viennese sentiment. D. L of C.

Poème, op. 17.

Manuel Ponce (b Fresnillo, Zacatecas, 1882; d Mexico City, 1948). According to Grove's Dictionary, "at his death he was recognized as the one Mexican composer whose music appealed to all levels of society." He performed as a pianist in the United States and

Europe. His sentimental songs and piano pieces were widely dispersed at one time.

Malgré tout (A Pesar de Toda): Danza. Repertorio Musical Menzel, 1900. An appealing tango, not hard. Slightly marred by "breaks" at the downbeats. 2 pp. NYPL.

Prelude and Fugue (1948). Editorial Cooperativa Inter-Americana. Very lyrical, almost classical harmony. An extended work, appealing and not difficult. Requires a working sostenuto pedal for a satisfactory performance. 12 pp. L of C.

Frank Addison Porter (b 1859). American

Etude mélodique, op. 33. Boston Music Co., 1922. Salon music, very sentimental. M-E. L of C.

Armand Qualliotine

Pezzi sinistre, 1989. *Rhapsody; Danza; Arabesque; Intermezzo; Paranoic Astral Dirge and Chant; Toccata.* Ms. Brandeis University.

Valentino Ragni

Mosaiken für 1 Hand. Zurich: Hug, 1982. 6 pieces in a contemporary idiom. (No. 1 is for right hand.) Includes a table of unconventional effects.

Dianne Goolkasian-Rahbee (b Somerville, Mass., 1938). Studied at the Juilliard School.

Abstracts, op. 7 (1970–81). Of these 9 short pieces, only No. 1, *Nocturne,* is for left hand alone. 1 p. M-E. Available from the composer: 45 Common St., Belmont, MA 02178.

Oreste Ravanello (b Venice, 1871; d Padua, 1938). Organist at San Marco, director of Instituto Musicale in Padua.

Variazioni in forma di esercizii sopra un tema di Domenico Scarlatti, op. 109. Milan: G. Ricordi, 1918. 16 short variations on the first eight measures of Scarlatti's Sonata in F minor, L. 383. As *esercizii* they are passable—arpeggios, thirds, leaps, and trills. But the music is disappointing, considering the superb theme Ravanello had to work with.

Jean-Henri Ravina (b Bordeaux, 1818; d Paris, 1906). French pianist, a prize-winning student at the Paris Conservatory. His elegant music had quite a vogue in its day. He published four-hand arrangements of all the Beethoven Symphonies.

Isolée!: Rêverie, op. 92. Mainz: Schott, c. 1883. Not important. M. G. Schirmer reprint (1915) at L of C.

Minnie Reese

Fantasy on Lily Dale. Nashville: Jesse French, 1874. Transcription. A poignant folk song which unfortunately does not quite come off in this impractical setting—the arpeggios are too big. L of C.

Max Reger (b Brand, Upper Palatinate, Bavaria, 1873; d Leipzig, 1916). German composer. In his Munich days he was a pianist of some renown, and he wrote many fugues for both organ and piano.

4 Spezialstudien. Leipzig: J. Aibl, 1902; Universal; also in "Lewenthal." 1. *Scherzo,* difficult opening (see Ex.49). 2. *Humoreske,* mostly staccato thirds, bright character;

D. 3. *Romanze,* very Brahmsian (with the characteristic Reger harmony), enriched at the return. 4. *Prelude and Fugue,* the best of the four, particularly the *Fugue* (see Ex.50). Without any special problems or learned devices, the counterpoint is very fine and feels good in the hand. At the end the *Fugue* opens up for excitement and then closes quietly. It may take a Reger "fan" to get really excited by all four works, but there is a serious musical approach, and the *Fugue* especially is very good. Recorded by Fred Moyer for GM Records: CD 2016.

EX. 49. Reger: *Scherzo* (Universal, 1902; reprint, Breitkopf & Härtel, 1957–1965), mm. 1–13.

EX. 50. Reger: *Fugue* (Universal, 1902; reprint, Breitkopf & Härtel, 1957–1965), mm. 18–19.

Carl Reinecke (b Altona, 1824; d Leipzig, 1910). Multifaceted German musician. He was close to Schumann, whose songs he arranged to the enthusiastic approval of the composer. Reinecke held two major posts—director of the Leipzig Conservatory and conductor of the Leipzig Gewandhaus concerts—and his role as guardian of the classical tradition shows strongly in his music. Liszt admired Reinecke's piano playing, and it was his piano works that brought Reinecke his greatest success as a composer.

Sonata in C minor, op. 179. Leipzig: C.F. Peters, 1884. The only other composer to publish a left hand sonata in the nineteenth century was Geza Zichy; it was not the age of the sonata and with a single hand it is hard to create the variety of texture necessary in a multimovement work. With his credentials Reinecke might have been the man for the job, but despite the great debt to Schumann and Brahms, his extreme conservatism can be almost maddening. Nothing is actually wrong musically, but he never "soars"; see Rheinberger and Hollaender for a finer rendering of this musical style. I. *Allegro moderato,* sonata form. II. *Andante lento;* this movement is the best, an appealing Hungarian tune— "Nemenj rózsám a tarlóra" followed by free variations (see Ex.51). III. *Menuetto:* both parts extensive. IV. *Allegro molto,* a good study in sixteenth-note passagework. IV in "Lewenthal."

2 Charakterstücke und eine Fuge, op. 1. Verlag Cranz.

Hugo Reinhold (b Vienna, 1854; d Vienna, 1935). Student of Bruckner at the Vienna Conservatory. Reinhold taught piano at the Akademie der Tonkunst Vienna and wrote attractively for his instrument.

EX. 51. **Reinecke:** *Sonata* (C.F. Peters, 1884), mvt. 2, mm. 1–6.

3 Etüden, op. 61. Vienna: Doblinger, 1907. *Tanz-Poem; Nocturne; Etüde.* The first two are fairly easy salon music, the third is more difficult. NYPL.

Anna Renfer

Klavierstudien, op. 37. Zurich: Kommissionsverlag Hug & Co. Despite the didactic title, this is a Baroque suite in contemporary guise: *Gaillarde; Rondeau; Allemande; Menuet; Sarabande; Bourrée; Air; Gigue.* Each movement maintains the traditional tempo and meter of the dance. Modest technical demands.

Emile Altner de Résimont

Redowa (Folk Dance), op. 6. Berlin: Otto Wernthal, n.d. Appealing. L of C.

Josef Rheinberger (b Vaduz, 1839; d Munich, 1901). As a renowned teacher of composition at the Munich Conservatory, Rheinberger counted among his students Humperdinck, Wolf-Ferrari, and Furtwängler. By age seven he was the organist at Vaduz. Today organists remember him for his twenty sonatas. Rheinberger was an outstanding composer who should not have fallen into obscurity. The problem lies with his archconservatism: he was a champion of the classical tradition and a staunch enemy of progress.

Capriccio, Menuetto und Fughetta, op. 133, no. 1. Munich: J. Aible, 1879. The *Capriccio* has some excitement (see Ex.52); the *Menuetto* is a good piece, but the *Fughetta* has no real counterpoint and is the least appealing of the set. Rheinberger's music has a good rhythmic and melodic profile, and, unlike the music of many other conservative Germans of the late nineteenth century, there is a fair amount of harmonic coloring. Very well written with regard to texture and use of the left hand. Joseffy Collection, University of Illinois at Champaign-Urbana.

EX. 52. **Rheinberger:** *Capriccio* (J. Aible, 1879), mm. 1–9.

Mazurka, Romance und Gavotte, op. 113, no. 2. Munich: J. Aibl, n.d. Technically quite
easy; the *Mazurka* is best.

Joseph Ricciardi and August Vella
Elementary Piano for One Hand. Boston Music Co., 1981. Good for beginners. 29 pp.

Alfred Richter (b Leipzig, 1846; d Berlin, 1919). Teacher and author of many music
textbooks.
Perpetuum Mobile, op. 3. Breitkopf & Härtel.

Alfred George Robyn (b St. Louis, 1860; d New York City, 1935). Organist at the Rialto
and Capitol Theaters, composer of many operettas.
Annie Laurie. St. Louis: Balmer and Weber Co., 1887. Transcription. M-D. L of C.

Eugénie R. Rocherolle (b New Orleans, 1936). Teacher in Wilton, CT.
Hands Separately. San Diego: General Words and Music Co., Kjos Music, 1989. Four
pieces: the two for left hand are the *Adagio* and the *Fantasia.* Nineteenth-century
in style, but elegant, with some appeal. Good for a not-too-advanced student.

Klara Rohmeyer
Intermezzo. Schanze: J. Akkorde, c. 1921.

J. Romano
Sextet from Lucia di Lammermoor, op. 206. Hutchings. Transcription from Donizetti's
opera. Brit. Lib.

Alfred Rose
Walzer, op. 9, no. 10. Berlin: Hoffheinz, c. 1901.

Daniel Rowe
March of the Midgets. Theodore Presser, 1915. A march for children. M-E. L of C.

Alec Rowley (b London, 1892; d London, 1958)
Colla Sinistra: 9 easy pieces for left hand. Rogers.

Franz Rubens
Caprice, op. 29. Berlin: Hoffheinz, c. 1906.

Adolf Ruthardt (1849–1915). German pianist and composer. Aside from his teaching
activities, he was an important editor associated with the Peters Editions.
Menuet, op. 47. Leipzig: Otto Forberg. c. 1906.
Studien und Stücke, op. 62. Leipzig: Otto Forberg, 1925. A big work with 21 exercises
and ten pieces, some of which are transcriptions from other composers. His original writing lacks musical interest, and the exercises are not up to those by Berens
and Phillip. NYPL.

Feliks Rybicki (b Warsaw, 1899). Composer and conductor; studied at the Warsaw
Conservatory, where he also taught. Awarded the Prime Minister's Prize in 1952 for his
works for young people.
Etiudy (Etudes), op. 54. Warsaw: Polskie Wydawnictwo Muzyczne. 3 vols. Vol. 1
(1962): 6 short pieces for children in a very traditional musical language. M-E.
Vol. II (1964); Vol. III (1965). M-D. L of C.

Louis Victor Saar (b Rotterdam, 1868; d St. Louis, 1937). After studies with Brahms, became an accompanist at the Metropolitan Opera in New York. Later he headed the Theory Department at Chicago Musical College.

Believe Me, If All Those Endearing Young Charms, 1933. Transcription.

Cora Sadler

On the Lake. New York: G. Schirmer, 1943. Elementary teaching material. L of C.

Camille Saint-Saëns (b Paris, 1835; d Algiers, 1921). For several decades one of France's major musical figures. He began as a phenomenal prodigy: at the age of ten he was offering to play as an encore any of the 32 Beethoven Sonatas! Throughout a long career as a pianist, he kept his wonderfully fleet fingers, while Liszt pronounced him "the greatest organist in the world." In his youth, Saint-Saëns championed the new music of Wagner and was the first in France to conduct Liszt's tone poems. But the later revolutions in music left him completely baffled—he ended up as an enemy of progress, pursuing an unfortunate vendetta against Debussy.

Six Etudes, op. 135. Paris: Editions Durand et fils, 1912. *Prélude; Alla Fuga; Moto Perpetuo; Bourrée; Elégie; Gigue. Moto perpetuo* in "Lewenthal." Most of Saint-Saëns' piano music stems from his latter years, and op. 135 represents the third and last time he grouped six studies together (the others were op. 52 and op. 111). Around 1900 Saint-Saëns' music took on an austere transparency, which the left-hand *Etudes* clearly evince. His use of the suite form attests to a lifelong interest in seventeenth-century French dance. One glance at this crystal-clear score—which owes as much to Rameau as it does to the Romantics—explains why, at the 1913 Paris première of Stravinsky's *Rite of Spring,* Saint-Saëns indignantly stalked out after the first few measures.

French pianist Robert Casadesus remembered his student days and the origin of the *Six Etudes:*

> And he [Casadesus' teacher, Louis Diémer (1843–1919)] was a very close friend of Saint-Saëns. I remember I played in Diémer's class one of the Saint-Saëns *Six Etudes* for the Left Hand. Saint-Saëns wrote these Etudes for the best pupils of Diémer. We were 12, so Diémer made the choice of six. I was what you call in French "chou-chou," the teacher's pet, so Monsieur Diémer gave me the sixth study, the Bourrée, the best piece of the set. I played it for Saint-Saëns, but I never spoke with him. And I never heard him play, unfortunately. [Interview with Dean Elder in *The Instrumentalist,* 1971.]

Anyone seeking that special brilliance Saint-Saëns conjured up in the finales of his piano concerti and in some other etudes will be disappointed, nor is there that great surge of melody to be found in his best pages. But within a chaste, almost rarified framework a first-rate musical mind is always in evidence. The title *Etudes* is a puzzle—the pieces are not difficult enough to justify it. The *Bourreé* has a refreshing quality (see Ex.53), and the *Perpetuo moto,* with its innocent wandering through nine keys, requires control (see Ex.2, p. 9). While a certain mildness of expression might mitigate against a complete performance, two or three selections may be effectively combined with Saint-Saëns' more brilliant studies.

EX. 53. Saint-Saëns: *Bourrée* (Durand et fils, 1912), mm. 1–8.

Gustave Samazeuilh (b Bordeaux, 1877; d Paris, 1967). French composer influenced by the early works of Debussy and Ravel. Perhaps more important as a writer and translator, he prepared the French versions of Wagner's *Tristan und Isolde* and Schumann's *Genoveva*.

Esquisses. Durand, 1948. Dedicated to Luciole. The *Sérénade* is for left hand. (*Souvenir* is for right hand.) Contrasting moods. M-D.

Pierre Sancan (b Morocco 1916). French, winner of the Prix de Rome and teacher at the Paris Conservatory.

Caprice Romantique. Paris: Durand & Cie., 1949. Dedicated to Madame Vosko-Chaki. A large-scale work, skillfully scored for one hand, in which the debt to Ravel's *Gaspard de la Nuit* and left-hand *Concerto* is clear. 9 pp. D. L of C.

Arnoldo Sartorio (b Frankfurt, 1853). German of Italian parentage, some of whose piano music became very popular.

Studies (1915), op. 1103. 12 pieces with Mendelssohnian harmony; none very difficult. Student works, pleasant and well written. 27 pp. NYPL.

10 Melodious Studies, op. 1136. Philadelphia: Theodore Presser, 1913. Easier and shorter than *Studies.* L of C.

Left Hand Proficiency: 23 original study pieces and transcriptions. Philadelphia: T. Presser, 1921. These are Sartorio's best works—fairly easy treatments of famous tunes from Wagner, Mozart, Gluck, Mendelssohn, and Schumann (*Träumerei*). Nicely scored, no awkward moments. L of C.

Souvenir de Handel, Introducing the Celebrated "Largo." Philadelphia: T. Presser, 1922. M-E. L of C.

Lovely Dorothea: Vien qui Dorina bella. Philadelphia: T. Presser, 1916. Straightforward transcription. L of C.

Emil Sauer (b Hamburg, 1862; d Vienna, 1942) German. One of Liszt's great pupils, he also studied with Nicholas Rubinstein and had a long career as performer and editor. His memoirs are entitled *Meine Welt*.

Waldandacht: Konzert-Etüde No. 28. Leipzig: B. Schott, 1917. Written for Count Geza

Zichy. Warm expression, beautifully scored, creating a good feeling in the hand. Quite ingenious in the difficult middle section, operatic in spots. Owes much to Schumann and Grieg. One of the best left-hand pieces from the Romantic period.

Maya Sauter (b Bienne 1910). Swiss pianist and composer.
Klaviermusik (1971). *Divertissements.* Zurich: Pelikan.
Improvisationen zum Transponieren, Nos. 4, 6, and 7. Zurich: Pelikan.
Ein- oder mehrstimmigen Studien, Nos. 2–6 and 9–12. Zurich: Pelikan.
Impromptus, Nos. 1 and 3. Zurich: Pelikan.

Robert Saxton (b London 1953). Head of composition at the Guildhall School.
Chacony (1988). Written for Leon Fleisher. "The title, an Anglicized variant of the French chaconne used by both Purcell and Britten, describes the basic idea of the music" (from the composer's program notes). 6 min.

A. Louis Scarmolin
Marigolds. Philadelphia: T. Presser, 1929. A simple *Andante;* acceptable "parlor" music. NYPL.

Franz Schmidt (b Pressburg, 1874; d near Vienna, 1939). Important Viennese composer, briefly a student of Bruckner. His opera *Notre Dame* brought him international fame for a time.
Toccata (1938) for piano or harpsichord. Vienna: Doblinger, 1978. One of his last works. Although an excellent pianist, Schmidt wrote little for the instrument until called upon by Paul Wittgenstein. Of the six pieces Schmidt wrote for his friend, this is the only one for solo piano—the others are concerted works and chamber music in a sensuous, Brahmsian texture. Here, the alternate scoring "for harpsichord" is significant: the dry Baroque feeling combines interestingly with a modern harmonic language and angular melodic shapes (see Ex.54). It was first published in a two-hand version by Schmidt's student Friedrich Wührer. D.

EX. 54. **Schmidt:** *Toccata* **(Doblinger, 1978), mm. 1–4.**

Jacob Schmitt (b Obernburg, Bavaria, 1803; d Hamburg, 1853). Reputable teacher and composer of over 370 piano pieces.

Etude de chant. In Ruthardt/Peters Album. Rather shallow music with many breaks in the melody. 4 pp. M-E.

Susan Schmitt

3 Easy Studies. Boston Music Co., 1921. 1. *The Merry Swiss Boy,* Old Folk Song; 2. *Barcarolle* ("Song of the Mermaids" from Weber's *Oberon*); 3. *Tom Thumb Waltz.* Easy music for a young student. L of C.

Peter August Schnecker (b Hesse-Darmstadt 1850; d New York City, 1903).

Romance in A-flat. Boston: O. Ditson, 1904. One of three he wrote for the left hand. M-E. No. 1 at L of C.

Schultz-Biesantz, editor

Album of Classical Piano Music—One Hand Alone: 17 Well-Known Pieces by Classical Composers, Arranged to be Played by Either Left or Right Hand. C.F. Peters.

Alexander Scriabin (b Moscow, 1872; d Moscow, 1915). Major Russian composer and pianist (see above pp. 5–6).

Prelude and Nocturne, op. 9. Leipzig: Belaieff, 1895. Also in "Lewenthal." Like his other early works, these pieces reveal the strong influence of Chopin and are far removed from the mystical style Scriabin evolved toward the end of his life. In every way these are the gems of the left-hand repertoire, and the *Nocturne* would probably be popular if it had been written for two hands. According to Detlev Kraus, who recorded them, they are based on two Russian folk songs: "I don't know why I'm so sad" and "Reverie under a birch tree."

The *Prelude* is much less known. These two poignant pages of Russian melancholy are considerably easier to play than the *Nocturne*, but the piece is in no way inferior to it. Though the opening can be sight-read easily enough, a perfect rendering of the second measure may prove elusive (see Ex.55).

EX. 55. Scriabin: *Prelude* (Belaieff, 1895), mm. 1–6.

The *Nocturne,* a memorable lyric outpouring, has a cleverly devised accompaniment, which rises to meet the melody and, in a few places, goes above it (see Ex.6, p. 10). The tricky cadenza is facilitated by sliding the thumb from D-flat to C (circled notes in Ex.56).

EX. 56. Scriabin: *Nocturne* (Belaieff, 1895), m. 27.

Gisela Selden-Goth (b Budapest, 1884). Hungarian writer and composer, a student of Bartók in 1907–1908. She wrote *The Life of Busoni* and edited his letters.

Quattro brevi studi. Tel Aviv: Israeli Music Publications, Ltd., 1958. Very challenging technically—true etudes. Many shifts of hand position, some counterpoint, syncopations. The slightly chromatic style resembles Busoni's. 10 pp. D. L of C.

Frank Shawcross

Nine Carols for Christmas (1985). *Nine More Carols for Christmas* (1986). Piano accompaniments arranged for one hand. Available from the Disabled Living Foundation.

Rennie Simmons

Three Little Dances for Left Hand Alone: Minuet, Gavotte and Musette, Gigue. Allan & Co.

Lucijan Marija Skerjanc (b Graz, 1900; d Ljubljana, 1973). Yugoslav composer, conductor, pianist, and writer on music.

Sest Klavirskih Skladb Za Eno Roko: 6 pieces for piano, one hand (1945). Slovenska Akademija, 1952. (Nos. 4, 5, and 6 are for right hand.) 1. *Etude:* difficult perpetual motion in 32nd-notes, wide spacings; 2. *Canzonetta:* an expressive *Andante;* 3. *Scherzo: Vivace,* challenging. Traditional tonality, well written and effective. 23 pp. L of C.

Nicholas van Slyck (b Philadelphia, 1922). Harvard-trained composer, student of Walter Piston.

Laments and Processional Music (1960). Long, multisectional, many tempos. 9 min. M-D.

Toccata (1967). 2 min. Ms. at American Music Center.

Gerrit Smith (b Maryland, 1859; d Connecticut, 1912). Celebrated organist. One of the founders of the American Guild of Organists, he taught at Union Theological Seminary.

Valse, op. 26. Arthur P. Schmidt, 1905. M-E. NYPL, L of C.

Sidney Smith (b Dorchester, 1839; d London, 1889)

Com'è gentil: Fantasy-etude on the melody by Donizetti. New York: G. Schirmer, 1869. Simply but awkwardly written. NYPL.

Warren Story Smith (b Brookline, Mass., 1885; d Boston, 1971). Music editor of *The Boston Post,* taught piano at the New England Conservatory.

Impromptu-Valse, op. 23. Arthur P. Schmidt, 1917. Nicely scored. L of C.

Léon Soli-Devère

Légende Livonienne. Brussels: Schott, c. 1889.

George Spaulding (b Newburgh, NY 1864; d Roselle Park, NJ, 1921). His thousands of works include many operettas.
1. The Artist's Dream. 2. Triumphal March. New York: Witmark & Sons, 1912. Easy and not significant. L of C.
Fairies' Nuptial March; Valse Sentimentale; Waltzing Nymphs. T. Presser, 1915.
Monarch Of All. T. Presser, 1917.

Alan Spencer (b Fair Haven, VT, 1870; d Chicago, 1950). For 20 years Dean of the American Conservatory.
Etude. Chicago: H.T. FitzSimons Co., 1935. Very fast and difficult; effective, with real sweep. 4 pp. Recommended.

Fritz Spindler (b Wurzbach, Lobenstein, 1817; d near Dresden, 1905). Active in Dresden. He published 330 works, some of which were popular in his day.
3 Romanzen, op. 156. Leipzig: Siegel, c. 1864. Reprint, Carl Fischer, 1910.
3 Brillante Klavierstücke: Ländler, Trauermarsch und Serenade, op. 350. Leipzig: Siegel, c. 1883.
3 Romanzen and Trauermarsch in Carl Fischer reprint at L of C; *Ländler* and op. 156, Nos. 2 and 3, at NYPL. All the works examined are of slight musical interest.

Charles Gilbert Spross (b Poughkeepsie, NY, 1874; d Poughkeepsie, 1961).
Album Leaf; Song Without Words. Cincinnati: John Church Co., 1913. Two pieces in a cloying style. L of C.

Alphonse Stallaert. Contemporary composer living in Paris.
2 Croquis. 1. Pour main gauche 2. Toccata.

Leon Stein (b Chicago, 1910). Dean of DePaul University School of Music, 1966–78.
Toccata No. 3, 1981. Commissioned by Norman Malone. Consists mostly of difficult *allegro* passagework in sixteenth notes. 5 pp. Ms. at American Music Center. Available from American Composers Edition, 170 W. 74 St. New York, NY 10023.

Eric Steiner
One Hand Only for the Young Pianist. Belwin-Mills.

W. Stepnitz
In The Greenwood: Valse-Idyll. Boston: Arthur P. Schmidt, 1922. Salon waltz. E. L of C.

Paul Stoye (b 1879; d Palos Verdes Estates, CA 1971).
Concert Valse. Des Moines: Youngman Music Co., 1925. This may be preferable to Godowsky's evocations of the Viennese waltz. The harmony is simple but authentic; flashy writing, not easy. Recommended. L of C.

Maurice Strakosch (b Gross-Seelowitz in Mähren, 1825; d Paris, 1887). Impresario and musician, a colorful figure active in New York City from 1848–60 as a teacher and pianist. He eventually gave up the piano to manage the singing career of his sister-in-law Adelina Patti. According to Arthur Loesser, the following satire in *The Knickerbocker* was written at Strakosch's expense. It is worth quoting as an example of that special brand of sly humor on which early American journalists seemed to have a monopoly:

Herr Smash began by raising his hands three feet above the keys, keeping them there for three minutes, then coming down with a furious crash that wrenched the brass plate off the piano and sent one leg scurrying across the floor. . . . Women waved handkerchiefs, infants bawled at the breast, sober men boohooed out of enthusiasm. The reporter glumly sucked his cane and applauded a little with his thumbnails. [*Men, Women and Pianos*, p. 390.]

Prayer From Rossini's Otello (Deh! Calma, o Ciel), op. 36. New York: W. Hall & Son, c. 1848. Desdemona's solo from the opera. Strakosch played this transcription at his Broadway Tabernacle recital in September 1849. Its impossible pile-ups of arpeggiated chords must represent something of a record.

Herman Strategier (b Arnhem, 1912). Dutch organist and composer, student of Andriessen, teaching at the conservatories of Utrecht and Rotterdam.
Tema con Variazioni (1959). In *6 Pieces for Left Hand by Dutch Composers*. Amsterdam: Donemus, 1963. A nice folklike tune in 5/8 time, followed by five short, free variations. M-D.

Soulima Stravinsky (b Lausanne, 1910). Son of Igor Stravinsky.
Sonatina Terza (1967). New York: Peters, 1975. The third movement, *Epilogue,* is for left hand. (The first is for right hand, the second for two hands.)

Joseph Strimer (b Rostov-on-the-Don, 1881; d New York City, 1962). Russian-American who studied with Rimsky-Korsakov and settled in New York.
Gavotte. Boston Music Co. 1953. Classical vocabulary, not engaging. M-E. L of C.

Felix Gerald Swinstead (b London, 1880; d Southwold, 1959). Professor at the Royal Academy of Music, toured the British Empire as a pianist. He wrote much piano music and a book on piano technique.
6 Studies for the Development of the Left Hand. London: W. Rogers, 1928. Only No. 1 (simple C major) is for left hand; the others are for two hands. L of C.

Jenö Takács (b Cinfalva, now Siegendorf, 1902). Austrian composer, pianist, and ethnomusicologist of Hungarian origin, student of Gal. He taught at the University of Cincinnati from 1952.
Toccata and Fugue, op. 56 (1950). Vienna: Doblinger, 1963. Begins as a paraphrase of Bach's *Chromatic Fantasy and Fugue* but has no connection to it after that. Very Baroque in texture; the *Fugue* is chromatic. It was engendered by a friend's inquiry as to whether it is possible to play with one hand alone. Takács mailed the piece to pianist Paul Wittgenstein, who (as usual) found it too modern and sent it back.

Wilhelm Tappert (b Silesia, 1830; d Berlin, 1907). Important Berlin teacher and Wagner enthusiast, editor of the *Allgemeine Deutsch Musikzeitung.*
50 Exercises. New York: G. Schirmer, 1892. A few are in "Lewenthal." Mostly quite short. Single and double notes; one note held, plus another voice; octaves. 37 pp. NYPL, L of C.

Wilhelm Taubert (b Berlin 1811; d Berlin 1891). Conductor, composer, and pianist; student of Ludwig Berger. Admired as a teacher by Mendelssohn. For twenty years he was the court Kapellmeister in Berlin. He wrote 300 songs, six operas, and much piano music.

Canzonetta in D-flat major. London, 1861.

Canzonetta in G: *Fata Morgana* No. 4, 1861.

These must be reprints, since according to Hofmeister's they were originally published before 1844. Brit. Lib.

Fritz Teichmann

Lyrische Stücke (Lyric Pieces) by Edvard Grieg, for left or right hand. Leipzig: C. F. Peters, c. 1911. A dozen transcriptions from Grieg's op. 12, op. 58, op. 65, and op. 68. L of C.

Gaetano Tesoriero

Bells. Australia: Albert Edition.

Charles Thibault (d 1853). A French-born pianist who taught in New York City from around 1818 to 1853. He claimed to be a prize-winner at the Royal Conservatory of France.

L'Ora Santa: Etude de Concert, op. 8 (c. 1828). Dedicated to Henri Herz. Mainz: Schott, c. 1846. A reprint of the first Paris publication. A very early left-hand work, intricate and extremely difficult, unusual for the inclusion of glissandi in thirds and sixths. L of C.

L'Invocazione: Etude Caractéristique de Concert, op. 9. Mainz: Schott, c. 1882. Also a reprint.

John S. Thompson (b Williamstown, PA, 1889). Settled in Kansas City and produced much teaching material for piano students.

For Left Hand Alone. Cincinnati: Willis Music Co., Book I, 1959; Book II, 1962. 20 simple and very agreeable children's pieces: traditional tunes, adaptations, and original melodies. Recommended.

William H. Thompson

Londonderry Air: Old Irish Melody. Philadelphia: T. Presser Co., 1943. Dedicated "To my pupil Gerald Peel." A sentimental arrangement. M-D. L of C.

John Tobin (b 1891; d Weston-Super-Mare, 1980). Conductor and Handel scholar.

One Hand Pieces (Left or Right): Prelude; Caprice; Barcarolle; Night March; Nocturne. London: J. Curwen; New York: G. Schirmer. Simple children's material. L of C.

Janoslaw Tomasek (b Korycany, Moravia, 1896; d Prague, 1970). Czech composer of the "Novak" group and a prolific writer.

Sonata, op. 7. Padua: G. Zanibon, date unclear. I. *Maestoso lugubre;* II. *Allegro appassionato.* Written for the composer's compatriot Ottaker Hollmann, a pianist injured in World War I. Contemporary style. 21 pp. D. NYPL.

Percy Turnbull (d Pulborough, England, 1976) Composer/pianist

Two Studies in Allemande Style. London: Augener, 1954. No. 1 is for left hand alone. Very Baroque in texture and musical feeling. M-D. L of C.

A.D. Turner
Four Melodious Studies, op. 29. Boston: A.P. Schmidt, 1884. Not too interesting. M-D.
L of C.

Paul Valdemar
Melody. Philadelphia: T. Presser, 1913. Cloyingly sweet. L of C.
Valse Caprice. T. Presser, n. d.

Grace Vamos American
A Memory. San Francisco: Grace Vamos, 1986. Easy broken chords, strange tonality.
2 pp. L of C.

Sidney Vantyn (1868–1937)
12 Etudes, op. 15. New York: M. August von Benham, 1895. Almost all are in single-
note passagework, No. 1 being the best (see Ex.57). L of C.
Finger Exercises, op. 16 no. 1; *Caprices,* op. 16 no. 2. New York: Carl Fischer; Berlin:
Schlesinger, 1894. A total of 5 in 14 pages; nothing special, two are good single-
note studies. M-D. Op. 16, no. 2 at L of C.

EX. 57. **Vantyn:** *Etude* (**M. August von Benham, 1895**), **mm. 1–2.**

Ranieri Vilanova
Romanza nell'opera Mignon dell Maestro Amb. Thomas. New York: R. Vilanova, 1877.
Rather difficult transcription, with octaves and fistfuls of chords. L of C.

Antha Minerva Virgil (b Elmira, NY; d New York City, 1945). Pianist/teacher.
In the Gloaming, op. 91. A.M. Virgil, 1922. Simple waltz.
The Wandering Fiddler, op. 98. A.M. Virgil, 1922. An imitation of simple violin music.
L of C.

Sotireos Vlahopoulos (b St. Louis, 1926). Former Head of Composition at Washington
Conservatory of Music.
Petite Sonatine. Written in 1986 for pianist/teacher George Kelver, who had been inca-
pacitated by a stroke. *Ronde; Serenade; Fugue.* Transparent textures, tonal; virtually
no counterpoint in the *Fugue.* 13 pp. M. Available from the composer: 657 Cyprus
Way East, Naples, FL 33942.

Axel Raoul Wachmeister (b London 1865; d Paris 1947) Swedish
3 Morceaux. Copenhagen: Wilhelm Hansen, 1929. Dedicated to Oscar Nissen. 1. *Glädje*
(Joie)—a slow C minor(!). 2. *Sorg* (Douleur); Adagio. 3. *Ateruppvaknande* (Reveil);
Allegro. Nos. 1. and 2 are somewhat like Sibelius; No. 3 is very simple. L of C.

Rune Wahlberg
Caprice. Edition Suecia Mansuskriptserien. Available from Swedish Information Center: Box 27 327, S-102 54, Stockholm.

Ernest Walker (b Bombay, 1870; d Oxford, 1949). He was instrumental in building the Music Department at Oxford University and gave the first English performance of several late pieces by Brahms.
Prelude, op. 61. London: Augener, 1935. Written for Paul Wittgenstein. *Larghetto,* rather easy, tonal. L of C.
Study For Left Hand, London: Augener, 1931. It is difficult to see how this layout of voices could have been conceived for one hand. 6 pp. L of C.

Johan Weegenhuise (b 1910)
Suite vour de Linkerhand. Amsterdam: Donemus, 1976. Copy of ms. *Allemande; Sarabande; Gavotte; Gigue*. All easy except the *Gigue*. Like so much contemporary Dutch piano music, it is dry and conservative in style. 8 pp. Northwestern University.

James M. Wehli
Home, Sweet Home. Boston: O. Ditson Co., 1870. A standard transcription, M-D. L of C .
Home, Sweet Home. Philadelphia: T. Presser, 1907. A second arrangement of the same song, this one a ferociously difficult virtuoso treatment. According to the title page it was "played at his concerts in America." L of C.

Arthur Henry West
Valse for Left Hand. London: Reynolds & Co., 1901. Brit. Lib.

June Weybright
Nocturne. New York: Belwin-Mills, Inc., 1954. Simple and naive, for youngsters. L of C.
To an Iceskater. Belwin-Mills Publishing Corp.

M. Wiggins
Midnight—Prelude for Left Hand. American Music Editions.

Philip G. Wilkinson (b London, 1929). Professor of Harmony and Composition at the Royal College of Music.
Suite: Left Hand Right Hand. London: Ascherberg, Hopwood & Crew, Ltd., 1966. Movements I, III, and V are for the left hand: *Polka; Minuet; Bourrée*. Good student material, M-D. NYPL.

Rudolf Willmers (b Berlin, 1821; d Vienna, 1878). Imperial and Royal Pianist.
Freudvoll und Leidvoll, by Reichardt, op. 2, no. 1. New York and Hamburg: Schuberth & Co., c. 1849. Transcription. The introduction to the reprint relates the story of Selma Franko, who played this piece when touring Europe and America as a child prodigy. L of C, NYPL.

August Winding (1835–1899). Director of the Copenhagen Conservatory.
Trois Morceaux, op. 27. Copenhagen: W. Hansen, c. 1888. *Capriccio; Canzonetta; Finale.*

His melodic gifts are disappointing, but the value lies in the technical demands of the long *Finale*. L of C.

Paul Wittgenstein (see above pp. 30–34)
School for the Left Hand, 3 vols. Vienna: Universal, 1957. After formative years in Vienna, this one-armed pianist had a long international career playing his commissioned concerti. Wittgenstein settled in New York City, where he taught extensively—at least two of his students were handicapped—and compiled this monumental collection.

Vol. 1: *Exercises.* Nearly 200, many of them real finger twisters, exhaustive explorations of a particular problem. There are 19 pages of double notes (see Ex.58). Wittgenstein enjoyed contrapuntal problems. These are very much "mental" exercises, and, as with many of the Godowsky *Paraphrases,* there is often a stimulating unfamiliarity to the patterns.

EX. 58. **Wittgenstein:** *Exercise* **1a (Universal, 1957).**

Vol 2: *Etudes.* These excerpts and rewritings from the two-hand repertoire are not music for performance, but elaborate exercises à la Phillip. Some Chopin *Etudes* are presented without the melody (see Ex.59).

EX. 59. **Chopin/Wittgenstein:** *Etude,* **op. 10, no. 12 (Universal, 1957), mm. 9–10.**

Vol. 3. *Transcriptions.* 27, including the actual music Wittgenstein played in his concerts. The choice of composers—Bach, Haydn, Mozart, Mendelssohn, Grieg, Schumann, and Wagner—reveals superior taste. Several are incredibly complex, actually being transcriptions of transcriptions, like the Bach/Brahms/Wittgenstein *Chaconne* and the Wagner/Liszt/Wittgenstein *Liebestod* (see Ex.16, p. 33). Coming from the pen of a veteran one-armed pianist, they contain some surprising miscalculations in the form of awkward breaks (see Ex.60). Wittgenstein was a literal transcriber, seemingly unwilling to rethink textures and accompani-

ments for this special medium. These arrangements could be made playable with a little rewriting. The Preface has a few remarks on playing and fingering left-hand music.

EX. 60. **Wagner/Wittgenstein:** *Quintet* **from** *Die Meistersinger* **(Universal, 1957), mm. 27–29.**

Bernhard Wolff (b Rakowitz near Schwetz, Prussia, 1835; d Berlin, 1906). A student of Hans von Bülow, author and an editor of many instructive works, including *The Little Pischna.*
Four Etudes, op. 257, no. 1. Boston: A.P. Schmidt, 1905. Not too interesting. M-D. L of C.

Sara Scott Woods
Waltz in A major, op. 39, no. 15, by Johannes Brahms. T. Presser, 1940. Well-written transcription. M. L of C.

Mary Wurm (b Southampton, 1860; d Munich, 1938). Successful English pianist and composer of German parentage, a student of Clara Schumann. Wurm founded and conducted an all-women's orchestra, which she took on tour from 1900.
Forty Daily Exercises. Leipzig: R. Forberg, 1911. Some are imaginative and rather difficult. They are placed at the very bottom of the keyboard, presumably because the action is heaviest there. Recommended. L of C.
Nocturne in E-flat, op. 9, no. 2., by Chopin. Leipzig: R. Forberg, 1911. A transcription scored in such a way that it might as well be for two hands. L of C.
Etude op. 42, no.1. Leipzig: Steingraber, c. 1906.
Lied ohne Worte, op. 51, no. 2.
Idylle, op. 51, no. 3.
Träler-Liedchen (Little Song), op. 51, no. 4. Leipzig: R. Forberg, 1911. Fairly easy, of slight interest. L of C.

Ruth Wylie (b Cincinnati, 1916). Flutist and composer; studied at the Eastman School.
Soliloquy, op. 23. Plainview, NY: Harold Branch Publications, Inc., 1966. ms.

Geza Zichy (Count) (b Sztára Castle, Hungary [now Czechoslovakia], 1849; d Budapest, 1924). (See above pp. 26–29.)
Sonata. Hamburg: D. Rahter, 1887. In three movements, with some uncomfortable scoring. The opening of the slow movement is not more playable by the left hand than a piano piece of Schubert (see Ex.61). Extremely conservative, simple harmony. 19 pp.

EX. 61. Zichy: *Sonata* (D. Rahter, 1887), mvt. 2, mm. 1–6.

Four Etudes (c. 1885). Reprint, Vienna: Universal, 1921. *Etude de concert; Capriccio; Allegretto grazioso; Wiener Spasse*. The last one is in "Lewenthal." His music offers some technical obstacles, but Zichy was a rather dull composer. These are fine historical curiosities, a chance to see what this one-armed pianist wrote for his own use in his European concerts of 100 years ago.

Six Etudes. Paris: Heugel, c. 1885. *Serenade; Allegro vivace; Valse d'Adèle; Etude; Rhapsodie Hongroise; Schubert's Erlkönig* (transcription). Preface by Franz Liszt, who later arranged *Valse d'Adèle* for two hands.

2 Morceaux. Paris: Durand et fils, 1886. *Sérénade; Divertimento. Sérénade* at L of C.

Fantasie über Motive aus R. Wagners Tannhäuser. Berlin: Adolf Furstner, c. 1883.

Chaconne in D minor from J.S. Bach's *Partita* in D minor for violin. Hamburg: D. Rahter, c. 1883.

Polonaise in A major, op. 40, no. 1, by Chopin. Budapest: Rossavolgyi & Co., c. 1883.

Hans Ziegler
Klage and Larghetto. In "Georgii."

Hermann Zilcher (b Frankfurt, 1881; d. Würzberg, 1948). Published over 100 works.
Präludium. In "Georgii." Warm lyricism, quite Brahmsian; well written. M-D.

7.

Solo Works for
the Right Hand Alone

Technical development, hand injuries, and virtuoso display are the three main inspirations for the vast left-hand repertoire. At the same time they explain the paucity of works for the right hand alone: The standard repertoire for two hands is already a gold mine of material for right-hand technical development; comparatively few pianists injure their left hands; and the right hand generally has the starring role, so a display by it would not have a dramatic impact. It is significant that only three works listed below were composed during the nineteenth century. Music for the right hand would result most naturally in the event of a particular artist's injuring his or her left hand. This happened to the British pianist Cyril Smith (b 1909), who had had a successful piano duet team with his wife, Phyllis Sellick. After suffering a thrombosis during a 1957 tour of the Soviet Union, he was no longer able to use his left hand. Courageously rebuilding their lives as a three-hand team, they received concerti for that medium from Malcolm Arnold, Arthur Bliss, and Gordon Jacob.

Actually, for those in need of material the repertoire for the right hand is potentially greater than it appears. A few minor works have been published under the more general headings "for one hand" and "for left or right hand." Some left-hand works can be transferred verbatim to the right: the three-hand concerti written for Smith and Sellick are now being played by Leon Fleisher and his wife, although Fleisher plays his part with the left hand. But truly idiomatic one-hand music usually requires some alterations in making the transfer, and many technical works—though they retain their musical meaning—lose their pianistic *raison d'être* if played by the other hand. For example, the Moszkowski *Etude* in G minor (see Ex.3, p. 9) would be of limited value to the right hand.

Jean Absil (b Bon-Secours, Hainaut, 1893; d Brussels, 1974)
Trois Pièces: Heroïque, Tendre, Gaie. For Franz Brown. Paris: Max Eschig, 1961. L of C.

Charles Valentin Alkan (b Paris, 1813; d Paris, 1888)
Introduction, variations et finale, op. 76, no. 2 (c. 1838). Paris: Editions M.R. Braun. The second of the *Trois grandes études.* University of Oregon.

Richard Rodney Bennett (b. Broadstairs, 1936). English composer and pianist.
Five Studies for Piano, No. 2. Universal, 1964.

Cathy Berberian (b Massachusetts, 1928; d Rome, 1983)
Moriscat(h)y. London: Universal, 1971. A musical joke, with the left hand miming the capture of a mosquito—that is, the buzzing of the right hand. The "author" must write a message and the code for translating it into notes and rhythms. NYPL Special Collections.

Marshall Bialovsky
C.P.E. Bach Comes to the American Southwest.
Two Meditations on Music of John Dunstable.
Twelve Variations on an Imaginary Jewish Folk Song.
Available from Sanjo Music, Box 7000–104, Palos Verdes Peninsula, CA 90274.

Allan Blank (b New York City, 1925). American composer and violinist.
Six Studies for Piano One Hand (Left or Right), Set 1, 1992. *Limited Shapes, Around Sustained Tones, Contrasts, Riding the Beat, Semi-Improvisation* (without barlines), *Serious Events.* Fast staccatos and passagework. 17 pp. D.
Six Studies for One Hand, Set 2, 1993. For right hand: I. *Staccato Sempre;* III. *The Ballerina's Flute Dance; V. Dramatic Fantasy.* (Nos. II, IV, and VI are for left hand.)
Both sets available from American Composers Editions, 170 W. 74 St., New York, NY 10023.

Paul Bliss (b Chicago, 1872; d New York City, 1933)
Two Compositions: Forest Echoes, The Winding Road. Philadelphia: T. Presser, 1926. 4 pp. E. L of C.

Ed de Boer (b 1957) Dutch
Toccata. Amsterdam: Donemus, 1978. 9 pp. D. Northwestern University.

York Bowen
Caprice from *Curiosity Suite,* op. 42. London: J. Williams.
Five Sketches. De Wolfe Ltd. Three are for right hand.

John Branson
Prelude. Cincinnati: Willis Music, 1989. 4 pp. L of C.

Louis Calabro (b New York City, 1926). Studied composition with Persichetti; at Bennington College from 1955.

Fantasy (1984). Written for Lionel Nowak. "The 'Fantasy' was composed with the thought of using the entire range of the piano. It deals with digital aspects in ways that I might not have considered when writing for the normal two hands. . . . The form of the piece is free and I just let my imagination roam" (L. Calabro). 6:24 min.

Tina Davidson (b Stockholm 1952). American, trained at Bennington College.
I Am the Last Witness (companion piece to *Day of Rage*, for two hands). Unpublished ms., 1984. Rhapsodic. 10 pp. M-D. American Music Center.

Auguste Dupont (b Ensival near Liège 1827; d Brussels, 1890)
Fantaisie et Fugue, op. 41. Mainz: Schott, c. 1875.

Ross Edwards. Australian
Three Little Piano Pieces. In "Australian." Tonal. 3 pp. E.

Brian Elias (b 1948) British
Five Piano Pieces. London: J & W Chester, Ltd., 1972. Very short and spare, atonal. Interesting widely spaced sonorities. Technically easy, but a musical challenge, with much rhythmic and dynamic detail à la Schoenberg.

Vivian Fine (b Chicago, 1913). Studied composition with Cowell and Sessions and taught at Bennington College from 1964 to 1987.
The Flicker (1973). Written for Lionel Nowak. "'The flight is deeply undulating, produced by several quick beats and a pause' (from Roger Tony Peterson's *A Field Guide to the Birds*). The bird song is also heard, and the flight and song intermingle" (V. Fine). 7:40 min.

Beatrice Hatton Fisk
A Right Hand Trick. New York: Schroeder & Gunther, 1944. A waltz. 2 pp. E.

Arthur Foote (1853–1937) American
Prelude-Etude, op. 37, no. 1. Boston: A.P. Schmidt, 1897. An arrangement of his *Etude* in D minor for left hand.

Peter Racine Fricker
Twelve Studies for Piano, op. 58, no. 5. Schott.

David Gallasch (b South Australia, 1934)
Space Music. In "Australian." 1 p. E.

Rudolf Ganz (b Zurich, 1877; d Chicago, 1972)
Capriccio, op. 26, no. 2. New York: G. Schirmer, 1917. In "Lewenthal." Gavotte-like. 7 pp. M-D.

Peter Golub
Six Pieces (1980). Written for Lionel Nowak. *Rhapsodically; Smoothly; Sprightly; Ringing; Majestically; Playful.* 5:46 min.

Cor de Groot (b Amsterdam, 1914)
"In Any Direction," A Poem for the Right Hand Only with 2 Pedals. Amsterdam: Donemus, 1974. 5 min. M-D.

Marjorie Hicks (b London, 1905) Canadian
2 Indispositions. Don Mills, Ontario: BMI Canada, Ltd., 1969. No. 2, *Indisposed Left Hand: Scherzino.* Energetic; fast, wide-ranging sixteenth notes; whole-tone formations. 3 pp. Excellent. (No. 1., *Indisposed Right Hand* is for left hand alone.) Eastern Illinois University.

Margriet Hoenderdos (b Santpoort, 1952). Dutch pianist and composer.
Es verjungt sich nach unten. Amsterdam: Donemus, 1986. 14 pp. 10 min. Northwestern University.

Henry Holden Huss (1862–1953)
Prélude No. 3 from *4 Préludes en forme d'études,* op. 17. New York: G. Schirmer, 1901. A gavotte in an innocuous conservative style. 3 pp. M-D.

Frank Hutchens (b Christchurch, 1892; d Sydney, Australia 1965). New Zealand composer who studied piano with Matthay in London.
Vienna Interlude: Piano Study (optional: both hands). Melbourne: Allan & Co., 1954. Nicely written. 6 pp. M.

Miriam Hyde (b Adelaide 1913) Australian
Three Studies. In "Australian." Written after breaking her left arm. 1. C minor; 2. *Staccato study;* 3. *Study on White Keys.* Challenging.
Poem (1973).

Ella Ketterer
Valse Melodique. T. Presser, 1951. A rudimentary waltz.

Karl Kohn (b Vienna, 1926). Teaches at Pomona College.
Etude for the Right Hand (and Foot), 1978. Written for Audrey Grigsby. Shifting meters, intricate. American Music Center.

Ellis B. Kohs (b Chicago, 1916)
Etude Variations on a Sestatonic Scale (A–B–C–D–D#–E) After a Theme by Johannes Brahms and E.B. Kohs' Fantasy II for Solo Violin. Ms., 1985. Tonal. 6 pp. M. American Music Center.
Ten Two-Voice Inventions, unpublished ms., (n.d.) Nos. 3 and 8 are for right hand. American Composers Alliance, 170 W. 74 St., New York, NY 10023.

Walter Lang (1896–1966) Swiss
10 Klavier-Etüden, op. 74. Hug, 1964. Only No. 4 is for right hand alone.

Elizabeth Lauer. American composer/pianist living in Wilton, CT.
Dextravaganza (1991). Written for her teacher Lionel Nowak, who for some years has
    been without the use of his left hand. Much of this ambitious work contains fast,
    etude-like quintuplet figures. Tremolos and repeated notes ("bebung"). Good use
    of the entire keyboard. Requires a working sostenuto pedal. 20 min. 17 pp. D.
    Available from American Composers Alliance, 170 W. 74 St., New York, NY 10023.

Jeffrey Leask (b Melbourne, 1944)
Film Theme. In "Australian." Easy traditional teaching piece. 1 p.

Cedric Wilmont Lemont
Valse in C major. Presser, 1929.

Jeffrey Levine
Soliloquy (1982). Written for Lionel Nowak. "Extracted from a set of variations, this
    piece could be described as a lyrical free fantasy on a compact motive" (J. Levine).
    5 min.

Otto Luening (b Milwaukee, 1900). Pioneer in electronic music and co-director of the
Columbia-Princeton Electronic Music Center, 1959–80.
The Right Hand Path (1984). Written for Lionel Nowak. "Built out of segments of the
    overtone row, which have various degrees of resonance depending on both spac-
    ing and the dynamics and sometimes the rhythm" (O. Luening). 5 min.

Wladyslawa Markiewiczowna
Przy Studni, No. 5, Etiuda Na Prawa Reke (By the Well). Kolobowe Obrazki, Zabrze:
    Dom Muzyki Polskies. C major. 1 p. M-E. (No. 4 is for left hand.) NYPL.

Harry Meyerowitz
Three Piano Compositions. New York: G. Schirmer, 1941. *Gavotte; Waltzing Snowflakes;*
    An Old Chinese Music Box. Easy instructional material.

Georges Migot (b Paris, 1891; d near Paris, 1976). French composer who was also a
successful painter, an instrument curator, and an author.
5 Etudes en forme de suite. Paris: Leduc, 1941. 12 pp. University of Arizona.

Allison Nowak (b Syracuse, 1948). American, studied with Fine and Calabro at Bennington College.
View for Right Hand (1981). "I wrote the 'View' as a gift to my father on his 70th birth-
    day in 1981. The 12-tone set on which it is based was originally created for an
    unfinished setting of Howard Nemerov's poem 'View from an Attic Window'" (A.
    Nowak). 6:40 min.

L. Augustus Nowak
Theme and Variations (1987). Written for Lionel Nowak. "My intention in writing the

Variations was to provide a traditional option in terms of tonality and phrasing to a repertoire that, from what I had heard, had tended to be more intricate and exploratory. I believe that the elementary lyric should maintain a segment of the spectrum in current composition" (L.A. Nowak). 7 min.

Lionel Nowak (b Cleveland, 1911). Composer and pianist at Bennington College. After suffering a stroke in 1980, he was restricted to using his right hand only. Works for his use came from 30 colleagues, eight of whom are associated with Bennington as faculty or alumni (see listings for Levine, Shawn, Fine, Luening, A. Nowak, L. Nowak, Golub, and Calabro). Lionel Nowak himself recorded their music; a cassette tape is available from Bennington College, Public Affairs Office, Bennington, VT 05201.

Practice Piece (1982). "Shortly after my stroke in spring, 1980, several composer friends signalled their sympathy by sending serious new scores for right hand alone. It occurred to me that certain finger and arm techniques were not in evidence so I decided to construct a piece for myself which could extend muscular facility by daily practice as warm-up" (L. Nowak). 2:29 min.

Marcello Panni (b Rome, 1940). Composer and active as a conductor in major opera houses.

Appunto 8.68. Milan: Edizioni Suvini Zerboni, 1972. A most interesting work in which the right hand plays a great many patterns and rhythms, all stemming from one initial chord of five unspecified white keys (see Ex.62).

EX. 62. **Panni: *Appunto 8.68* (Zuvini Zerboni, 1972), mm. 1–9.**

Felix Petyrek (1892–1951) Austrian
Zwei Tanzstücke. In "Georgii."

Robert Pollock (b 1946)
Short Study. Ship Bottom, NJ: Association for the Promotion of New Music, 1979. 3 pp. 2 min. NYPL.

Valentino Ragni
Kleine (Petite) Rhapsodie, No. 1 from *Mosaiken*. Zurich: Hug, 1982. Contemporary notation. M.

Eugénie R. Rocherolle. American, raised in New Orleans, now living in Wilton, CT, where she teaches piano.
Etude; Waltz. From *Hands Separately* (contains 4 pieces). San Diego: General Words and Music Co., Kjos Music, distributor, 1989. Nice turn-of-the-century old-fashioned style; elegant. Some challenges.

Ned Rorem (b Richmond, IN, 1923). Prominent American composer, on the faculty of the Curtis Institute.
Eight Etudes for Piano. No. 7 is for right hand. Boosey & Hawkes, 1975.

Gustave Samazeuilh (1877–1967) French
Souvenir. Paris: Durand, 1948. The second of *2 Esquisses*. (The *Serenade* is for left hand.)

Maya Sauter (b Bienne, 1910). Swiss pianist and composer.
Improvisationen zum Transponieren, Nos. 1 and 3. Pelikan.

Allen Shawn (b New York City, 1948). Pianist and teacher at Bennington College.
Six Miniatures (1988). Written for Lionel Nowak. *Majestic and singing; With driving rhythm; Con brio; Molto tranquillo e espressivo; Brittle, angry; Maestoso, freely*. "The harmonies of the opening chorale are echoed in No. 4, and form the basis of the cadenza-like sixth movement. Though also linked to the chorale, the remaining pieces provide contrast; numbers 2 and 3 are balletic in character, and No. 5 is a rather acerbic march" (A. Shawn). 10:25 min.

Lucijan Marija Skerjanc (1900–1973) Yugoslavian
Six Pieces. Ljubljana, 1952. Nos. 1, 2, and 3 are for right hand: *Preludio; Quasi Valse; Toccatina*. No. 3 is the most interesting.

E. De Santa Sourget
Gavotte Variée. Brussels: Schott, c. 1881.

Soulima Stravinsky (b Lausanne, 1910). Son of Igor Stravinsky, with whom he performed frequently on two pianos.
Piano Suite for the Right Hand (1975). New York: Peters, 1980. Dedicated to the memory of Walter Hinrichsen. *Prelude; March; Waltz; Gavotte; Sarabande; Gigue*. Serial technique, with the 12-tone row spelled out at the beginning ("Symbol—not to be played"). Bare textures. E.
Sonatina Terza (1967). New York: Peters, 1975. The first movement, *Fantasia piccola*, is for the right hand (the second movement is for two hands, the third movement for left hand).

Yuji Takahashi (b Tokyo, 1938). Japanese composer and accomplished pianist; a student of Xenakis, learned computer music in New York City.

3 Poems of Mao Tse-tung. Japan: Zen-On Music, 1976. The first two, *Tapoti* and *Ode to the Plum Tree,* are sparely written in the treble clef and, though the score does not specify it, are clearly for the right hand alone. The third piece, *Reply to Corirade Kuo Mo-Jo,* requires two hands. Without barlines, moderate tempos and very simple rhythms, some large arpeggios. The score contains Mao's poetry in Chinese, Japanese, and English. 6 pp. M. Southern Baptist Theological Seminary.

Gunther Tautenhahn
Bagatelle. New York: Seesaw Music Corp., 1976. California State University at Fullerton.

Philip E. Wilkinson (b London, 1929)
Suite: Left Hand, Right Hand. London: Ascherberg, Hopwood & Crew, Ltd., 1966. Nos. 2, 4, and 6 are for right hand: *Pavanne; Fughetta; Jig.* Good student pieces. M.

Mary Wurm (b Southampton, 1860; d Munich, 1938)
Etude, op. 42, no. 2. Leipzig: Steingraber, c. 1905.

8.

Works for One Hand and Orchestra

PIANO LEFT HAND AND ORCHESTRA

Arnold Bax (b Streatham, 1883; d Cork, 1953)
Concertante. Chappell, 1949. Originally titled *Concerto*. His last important work, written for British pianist Harriet Cohen (1895–1967). This dear friend of Bax had suffered a permanent injury to her right hand the previous year, when a glass she was holding suddenly shattered. She played left-handed for a few years, reluctantly retiring in 1961. Neo-classical in style. Three movements. 24 min.

Sergei Bortkievicz (b Kharkov, 1877; d Vienna, 1952)
Concerto No. 2, op. 28. Written in 1930 for Paul Wittgenstein. Unpublished ms. at NYPL.

Rudolf Braun (1869–1925). Blind organ virtuoso and teacher of composition in Vienna.
Concerto in A minor. Universal, 1927. Written for Paul Wittgenstein.

Benjamin Britten (b Lowestoft, 1913; d Aldeburgh, 1976)
Diversions, op. 21 (1940; revised, 1954). London: Boosey & Hawkes, 1955. Dedicated to Paul Wittgenstein and first played by him with the Philadelphia Orchestra and Eugene Ormandy in 1942. Britten came to the United States in the summer of 1939, disheartened by the Spanish Civil War and other political events in Europe. Among several major works from his American stay was *Diversions*, written in Maine. Wittgenstein was also in the United States as a recent emigré, and Britten admired his courage in the battle to master the piano one-handed. The commis-

sion attracted him immediately, though it seems he was later disenchanted by the liberties Wittgenstein introduced into his performances.

Diversions holds ten clever variations on a theme, each with its own title and distinct mood. The composer wrote:

> In no place in the work did I attempt to imitate a 2-handed piano technique, but concentrated on exploiting and emphasizing the single line approach. . . . Special features are trills in the *Recitative*, widespread arpeggios in the *Nocturne*, agility over the keyboard in the *Badinerie* and *Toccata*, and repeated notes in the final *Tarantella*.

Britten quite understates the formidable technical difficulties: *Diversions* requires superb technique and benefits (at least in *Toccata I*) from a very large hand.

C. Curtis-Smith (b Walla Walla, WA, 1941). Prize-winning composer, teaching at Western Michigan University.
Concerto. Commissioned for Leon Fleisher by the Irving S. Gilmore Keyboard Festival and premiered there by Fleisher in 1991. I. *Lento agitato—Allegro con fuoco;* II. *Larghetto;* III. *Moto perpetuo:* "Brilliant and ringing!" According to the composer,

> the timbral metaphor of the Concerto is the sound of a struck bell. In the beginning, the piano's rolling B-flats, tolling as a bell, give rise to the themes and motives of the Concerto. . . . The bell metaphor becomes more literal in the third movement. Here, the melodic material is based on the English tradition of change ringing.

Norman Demuth (b Croydon, 1898; d Chichester, 1968). English composer and writer on music.
Concerto, 1947. Unpublished.
Legend, 1949.
Both works composed for Paul Wittgenstein.

Cor De Groot (b Amsterdam, 1914)
Variations-Imaginaires. Henmar Press, 1962. *Introduction; Nocturne; Scherzo; Quasi Walzer; Burlesque; Evocation; Finale; Presto.* Tonal contemporary harmony; some early parts difficult: simple rhythms. 22 min. Ms. of 2-piano score in NYPL.

Paul Hindemith (b Hanau, near Frankfurt, 1895; d Frankfurt, 1963). Major German composer.
Klaviermusik (Concerto), op. 29. Written in 1923 for Paul Wittgenstein, who never performed it. Never published, and the manuscript is lost.

Leonard Kastle (b New York City, 1929). Studied composition with George Szell and piano with Isabella Vengerova.
Concerto. Written for Paul Wittgenstein.

Erich Korngold (b Brno, 1897; d Hollywood, 1957)
Klavierkonzerte in C-sharp, op. 17. Mainz: Schott, 1923. Written for Paul Wittgenstein,
who played it in 1924. Maurice Hinson writes "Korngold's warm, sumptuous Ro-
manticism comes through brilliantly. Lyrical richness sometimes reminds us of R.
Strauss or even G. Mahler. M-D."

Joseph Labor (1842–1924). Viennese, blind from birth. Composition teacher of
Wittgenstein and Schoenberg.
Concert Piece in the Form of Variations (1916). Wittgenstein made his return to the con-
cert stage with this work.
Concert Piece in B minor (1936).
Concert Piece in F minor (1936).

Kurt Leimer (b Wiesbaden, 1920; d 1974). Led the piano master classes at the Salzburg
Mozarteum. Strauss so admired Leimer that he awarded this pianist exclusive performance rights to the *Panathenäenzug* for several years. (Note, however, Leimer's poor LP
recording of that work, with many simplifications.)
Concerto in one movement (unpublished?). Premiered under Herbert von Karajan and
the Vienna Philharmonic in 1953.

Bohuslav Martinů (b Policka, east Bohemia, 1890; d Liestal, Switzerland, 1959). One
of the most prolific Czech composers, a figure of international standing during the last
decades of his life.
Concertino (Divertimento) for Piano and Chamber Orchestra (1926). Bärenreiter. Written
for compatriot Otakar Hollmann (1894–1967), who lost the use of his right arm
during World War I. I. *Allegro moderato*; II. *Andante*; III. *Allegro con brio*. Neo-
classical, very clear rhythms in outer movements, cadenza in the last. The lovely
extended piano passage which opens the *Andante* could be extracted as a solo
piece.

Sergei Prokofieff (b Sontsovka, Ekaterinoslav district, Ukraine, 1891; d Moscow, 1953)
Concerto No. 4 in B-flat, op. 53 (1931). International Music Co., 1961. Written for Paul
Wittgenstein, whose rejection of the Concerto was described by Prokofieff in his
"Autobiographie":

> When I sent my Concerto to Wittgenstein, he wrote: "I thank you for the Concerto,
> but I don't understand one note of it and will never play it!" And so the Concerto has
> never been played up to the present. I myself have come to no definite opinion about
> it—sometimes it pleases me, sometimes not, and I should decide to make a two-hand
> arrangement of it. The construction is as follows: I. In fast tempo, generally based on
> finger technique; II. Not without a certain peaceful discretion; III. In the manner of a
> Sonata allegro although deviating from it; IV. A reminiscence of the first movement,
> only shortened and piano throughout. [*Sergei Prokofieff: Dokumente, Briefe, Errinerun-
> gen*, translated from the Russian by Felix Loesch (Leipzig: VEB Deutscher Verlag für
> Musik, [1965?]).]

Wittgenstein never did play the work, nor did Prokofieff arrange it for two hands. But the German pianist Siegfried Rapp, who lost his right arm in World War II, obtained the score and gave the first performance in 1956, a quarter of a century after its creation.

The rejection of the work by Wittgenstein was probably based on his extreme musical conservatism—he was, as he admitted, a musician of the nineteenth century. However, despite its reasonable technical demands, this piece has never been popular with other performers. It sounds uninspired and cannot be seriously compared with earlier concerti by Prokofieff for character, melodic inspiration, color, and excitement—in short, all the qualities which earned him his special place in twentieth-century music.

Maurice Ravel (b Ciboure, Basses Pyrénées, 1875; d Paris, 1937)
Concerto in D. Paris: Durand (1937). Written for Paul Wittgenstein in 1930. One of Ravel's masterpieces and the absolute summit of the left-hand repertoire (see pp. 32–33). It was written concurrently with the G major *Concerto*, and nothing could be farther removed from its sparkling Mozartean sound world than this dark and fateful music. Together the *Concerti* constitute the two poles of Ravel's persona; and they are his last compositions for the piano.

Ravel prepared extensively for his task by studying the left-hand works of Saint-Saëns, Godowsky, Scriabin, Czerny, and Alkan. This work is in one large ternary-form movement. The opening seems to rise out of the very depths of the orchestra, with the piano solo continuing the fateful mood. The extended middle section, in a driving 6/8, ranges from playfulness to savagery and incorporates a distinct jazz element. The *Concerto* is remarkably eclectic, mixing Spanish traits, polytonality, jazz, and Impressionism—one copy of the manuscript bears the words "musae mixtatiae" (mixed muses). The technical demands are extreme, not least being the projection of the cadenza's melody over its swirling accompaniment.

Ned Rorem (b Richmond, IN, 1923). Prominent American composer, on the faculty of the Curtis Institute.
Concerto No 4. Boosey & Hawkes. Written for pianist Gary Graffman, who has been unable to perform professionally with his right hand since 1980 because of (in his words) "the inability to control the fourth and fifth fingers when playing certain passages". Graffman, Director of Curtis, premiered it at the school in February 1993, with André Previn conducting. Rorem has written: "Perhaps 'Concerto' is too grand a title, connoting as it so often does a virtuosic struggle between soloist and orchestra. Rather, this is an 'entertainment,' shaped like a suite." Graffman described the work in detail:

> The piece is in eight short movements, channeled into three larger sections, but the whole thing is played almost without pause. It's a bit over half an hour. Although the work is based on a twelve-note motif, which I start off playing alone ("like sparks," according to the score), it is tonal and melodic. The first section contains three rapid, glittering movements—*Opening Passacaglia*, *Tarantella* and *Conversation*. The second, slow and moody, invokes Rorem's song-writing gifts, with a chorale-like *Hymn* accompanied by all the violins in unison; a *Duet*, with an extended 'cello solo; and a

Vignette, where I play a childlike tune, accompanied this time by very adultlike syncopated winds. . . . The last section begins with *Medley*, a free-form piano cadenza, which merges, after a cosmic fortissississimo (yes, five *fffffs*), into a ground-bass, proclaimed and insisted upon throughout this *Closing Passacaglia* by the timpani, growing gradually from a whisper (the score says, "through the mist") to a roar. [*Keyboard Classics and Piano Stylist*, March/April 1993.]

Franz Schmidt (b Pressburg, 1874; d Perchtoldsdorf, 1939)
Concertante Variationen über ein Thema von Beethoven (1924). Original version for left hand. Published in ms. Vienna: Georg Kugel, 1926. Version for two hands by Friedrich Wührer. Universal, 1953. 26 min.
Klavierkonzerte (1935). Original version for left hand. Published in ms. Copy given to Vienna State Library by Wittgenstein in 1950. Version for two hands by Friedrich Wührer. Universal, 1955. 38 min.

Eduard Schütt (1856–1933) Austrian, born in Russia.
Paraphrase. Performed in 1929 by Paul Wittgenstein. Unpublished?

Lucijan Marija Skerjanc (1900–1973). Yugoslavian, born in Austria.
Concerto (1963). Ljubljana S.A.Z.U., 1967. I. *Lento;* II. *Calmo e sentito*; III. *Moderato rapsodico—allegro ruvido.* Richly written, fairly tonal. D. NYPL, L of C.

Richard Strauss (b Munich, 1864; d Garmisch-Partenkirchen, 1949)
Parergon zur Symphonia Domestica, op. 73. London and New York: Boosey & Hawkes, 1964. First played by Paul Wittgenstein in Dresden, under Fritz Busch, 1925. According to Norman Del Mar (*Richard Strauss, a Critical Commentary on his Life and Works* [Philadelphia: Chilton Book Co., 1969]), Strauss often stayed with his friends the Wittgensteins in Vienna. On one such occasion, Paul took the opportunity of asking his guest for a concerto. Strauss responded a few years later by giving musical expression to an event from his own family life, the serious illness and recovery of his son Bubi. "Parergon" means "off-shoot" or "companion-piece," and this concerto is dominated by Bubi's theme from Strauss's autobiographical *Sinfonia Domestica.* Actually, Strauss could only refer briefly to his own theme, for fear of accusations of copyright infringement from his publisher! A threatening C-sharp serves as an *idée fixe,* while F major represents a return to normalcy.
    Parergon is a multisectioned, one-movement work, with extremely difficult cascades, chords, and scales. The soloist plays almost continually, battling a very thick orchestra part, though most of the pianist's efforts would inevitably be covered by the orchestra. 106 pp., 18 min.
    Parergon was recorded by Hilde Somer, with the San Antonio Symphony conducted by Victor Alessandro. Mercury SR 90517; LP at NYPL.
Panathenäenzug: Sinfonische Etüden in Form einer Passacaglia, op. 74. Boosey & Hawkes, 1953. 25 min. Played in 1928 by Wittgenstein, under Franz Schalk and the Vienna Philharmonic. Wittgenstein had enjoyed his first collaboration with Strauss, though he claimed the balance between orchestra and piano had worked against him. This time Strauss went to ancient Greece for his inspiration:

The Panathenäenzug was the great annual festival of ancient Athens, every fourth year of which worked up to the climax of a brilliant procession. The occasion being the supposed birthday of the goddess Athena, not only youths, maidens, sacrificial animals, chariots and cavalry took part in the procession, but an elaborately embroidered robe for her personal use—known as a peplos—was hoisted to a ship on wheels and trundled through the city. . . . The whole magnificent affair is the subject of a frieze on the Parthenon. [Del Mar, p. 291.]

The Introduction is followed by an unbroken set of variations over a continuously repeating ground bass. "The Panathenäenzug falls into four main sections, with introduction, two interludes and coda, thus also emulating the Lisztian one-movement sonata which Strauss had already followed in so many of his previous symphonic works" (Del Mar, p. 291).

The colors of the lyra (a kind of glockenspiel), the celeste, and the harp are effective in spots. Again, as in *Parergon*, the endurance test is grueling, the difficulties hair-raising. But the digital activity exceeds the actual musical inspiration, leaving an effect of note-spinning, and this is one of Strauss's least-performed scores. With the exception of the early *Burleske*, these are the only piano concerti he wrote.

Panathenäenzug was recorded by Kurt Leimer, with the Nuremburg Symphony Orchestra conducted by Gunther Neidlinger. Leimer simplified many passages and played his own cadenza.

Alexander Tansman (b Lodz, Poland, 1897). Polish composer and accomplished pianist, active in Paris, worked in Hollywood on film scores.
Concert Piece (c. 1943). Written for Paul Wittgenstein.

Karl Weigl (1881–1949). American, born in Austria.
Concerto (1924). *Allegro* (with cadenza); *Adagio; Rondo.* 18 min. American Composers
    Alliance.

Geza Zichy (see above, pp. 26–29)
Konzert in E-flat major. Hamburg: Rahter, c. 1900; New York: G. Schirmer, 1895; large
    print: Albert J. Gutmann. 3 movements. History's first work for piano left hand
    and orchestra.

PIANO RIGHT HAND AND ORCHESTRA

Henri Cliquet-Pleyel (b Paris, 1894; d Paris, 1963). French composer, a student of Gédalge, and close to *Les Six*.
Concerto. Jobert. 21 min.

PIANO THREE HANDS AND ORCHESTRA

The following works by British composers Arnold, Bliss, and Jacobs were written for the duo-piano team of Cyril Smith and Phyllis Sellick (see above, p. 100).

Malcolm Arnold (b Northampton, 1921)
Concerto for Phyllis and Cyril, op. 104, for 2 pianos, 3 hands (1969). G. Schirmer. A short and joyful work; diatonic.

Arthur Bliss (b London, 1891; d London, 1975). British composer of American descent; Master of the Queen's Music for 22 years.
Concerto for 2 pianos, 3 hands, op. 17 (1968). A revision of his 1924 *Concerto* for 2 pianos.

Gordon Jacob (b London, 1895; d Saffron Walden, 1984)
Concerto. Novello, 1969. 20 min.

Gunther Schuller (b New York City, 1925). Significant American composer, conductor, and educator. President of the New England Conservatory, 1966–77. Important in establishing a link between serious music and jazz, he launched the slogan "Third Stream."
Concerto for 3 hands. Written for Lorin Hollander and Leon Fleischer on a commission from the Springfield Symphony Association. Premiered in 1990 by those two artists with the Illinois Chamber Orchestra conducted by Kenneth Kiesler. 20 min.

> The work is in five movements, all performed without pause. The movements are distinguished from one another not only by substantial contrasts in mood, character and tempo, but instrumentation as well. The two pianists are accompanied in the five movements first by percussion alone, in the second movement woodwinds, in the third strings, the fourth brass, and in the fifth movement, at the very end, the full orchestra . . . . The fifth movement is in effect a cadenza for the left-hand pianist. [From the composer's program notes.]

9.

Chamber Music

FOR PIANO AND OTHER INSTRUMENTS

Miguel del Aguila (b Montevideo, 1957). American composer/pianist.
Fantasie for cello and piano, op. 10 (1986). Freely atonal, multisectional, many tempo
and character changes; strong rhythms, interesting and very fast unison passages,
good interplay between instruments. Exciting. M-D. 8 min.
Burlesque for flute and piano (1987). An adaptation of the *Fantasie*. Available from the
composer: 215 Thomas Ave., Oxnard, CA 93033.

Michael Appleton
Sonata for viola and piano in G minor. Anglian New Music.

Walter Bricht (b Vienna, 1904; d Bloomington, IN, 1970). In the United States from
1938, later a Professor at Indiana University.
Variations on a Folk Song for piano, flute, and cello, c. 1942. Written for Paul Wittgenstein, unpublished.

Louis Calabro (b New York City, 1926). Studied composition with Persichetti; at Bennington College from 1955.
In(ter)vention. For piano right hand and timpani. Written for Lionel Nowak.

Hans Gal (b 1890, near Vienna; d Edinburgh, 1987). Important Viennese composer and musicologist who fled from the Nazis to Scotland. He wrote half of his works there and was the author of several books on composers.
Piano Quintet in A. Performed by Wittgenstein in 1928.
Piano Quartet in A, op. 13. (May be the same work as the *Quintet*.)

Leos Janáček (b Hukvaldy, Moravia, 1854; d Moravská Ostrava, 1928). Recognized as one of the most substantial Czech composers of the century, particularly in the domain of opera.
Capriccio for Piano and Winds (1926). Prague: Státní nakladatelství krásné literatury, hudby a umení, 1959. For flute/piccolo, 2 trumpets, 3 trombones, tuba, and piano. Written for Czech pianist Otakar Hollmann, whose right arm was completely paralyzed after he served at the front in World War I. Janáček was at first reluctant to write for Hollmann, perhaps because of his own lack of enthusiasm for the piano generally. Hollmann played this unusual work for the first time in 1928. It was the last première of his own music that Janáček ever attended, for he died that same year.
　　The original title, "Defiance" (which does not appear in the score), may express the composer's feelings for Hollmann's tragic fate. However the music itself, though strongly characterized, is far from tragic. Some commentators consider the work a failure because of its scoring: the low brass are lugubrious and unwieldy in spots, and the flute sounds awkward in this ensemble. The piano writing is stark and far from easy, although many of the difficult passages have simplified *ossias*. While the texture takes getting used to, the work has its rewards. It is in four short movements: *Allegro; Adagio; Allegretto; Andante*. The highlight is the *Adagio,* a touching, mosaic-like movement built up from a few simple melodic ideas.

Ernst-Lothar von Knorr (b Eitorf, 1896)
Intermezzo for piano and violin. In "Georgii."

Erich Korngold (b Brno, 1897; d Hollywood, 1957). After a career as a phenomenal prodigy in Vienna, climaxed by the success of his opera *Die tote Stadt* at age 20, Korngold came to the United States, where he achieved success as a composer of film scores.
Suite for 2 violins, cello, and piano, op. 23. Mainz: Schott, 1930. I. *Prelude* (begins with Piano alone) *and Fugue;* II. *Waltz;* III. *Groteske;* IV. *Lied;* V. *Rondo finale.*
Piano Quintet in E major, op. 15, 1924.
Both works were written in Vienna for Paul Wittgenstein.

Joseph Labor (1842–1924). Austrian composer and pianist, blind from childhood. He was the composition teacher of Paul Wittgenstein, for whom he wrote the following works. All are unpublished.
Quartet No. 2 in C minor, op. 6. Performed 1917.

Sonata in G for piano and violin. Performed 1917.
Divertimento for piano, flute, oboe, and viola. Performed 1932.
Trio for piano, clarinet, and viola. Performed 1932.
Piano Quintet in D, op. 11, n.d.
Piano Quintet in E minor, op. 3, n.d.

Franz Schmidt (b Pressburg, 1874; d Perchtoldsdorf, near Vienna, 1939). Major Austrian composer, and an excellent pianist trained by Leschetizky. Fame came to him with his opera *Notre Dame.*

The Quintets of Schmidt are exceptionally beautiful, real gems of the late-Romantic repertory. In general they represent the lyrical, introspective side of his musical personality, but there are powerful moments too. Schmidt had the eloquence and imagination of a first-rate composer, and the string writing is full and sensuous, reminiscent of Brahms. The writing for piano, though subtle, is not in virtuoso style, but impressionistic and delicate. Schmidt's treatment of the keyboard is not the concerted opposition to the strings found in some Romantic chamber music; rather, the piano is highly integrated into the overall texture. There is much filigree, with harp- and celeste-like effects. Schmidt's three Quintets were commissioned and performed by the composer's friend Paul Wittgenstein—the scores bear a dedication to him. But it seems that only the first, in G major, was ever published in its original one-hand version. Wittgenstein premiered the first two quintets, but by 1939, he had already emigrated to America.

Quintet in G major for 2 violins, viola, cello, and piano. Edition 1, for left hand. Vienna: Georg Kugel, 1927 (private printing). L of C. Edition 2, for left hand. Vienna: Waldheim-Eberle. Edition 3, for two hands. Version by Friedrich Wührer, Vienna: Josef Weinberger, 1944.

Quintet in B-flat major for clarinet, violin, viola, cello, and piano. Two-hand version by Friedrich Wührer, Vienna: J. Weinberger, 1954.

Quintet in A major for clarinet, violin, viola, cello, and piano. Two-hand version by Friedrich Wührer, Vienna: J. Weinberger, 1954. Just after Schmidt's death, Friedrich Wührer gave the first performance of the A major *Quintet* in his own two-hand arrangement. This work differs formally from the others. The fifth movement is a set of variations on a theme by Josef Labor. Wittgenstein had been a student of Labor in his youth, and Schmidt thought that the pianist would enjoy this tribute to his teacher. The *Variations* were long enough for Wittgenstein to perform them as an independent work in his American concerts. Also unusual is the insertion of an *Intermezzo* for solo piano. At first Wittgenstein was nervous about his solo, thinking the other players would resent this unprecedented spotlighting of the pianist, but his fears were unfounded.

Pianist Jorg Demus and his colleagues have recorded the Quintets outstandingly well on the Electrola label, and listeners unfamiliar with this unjustly neglected composer have a wonderful surprise in store. The problem for left-hand performers is the unavailability of the one-hand versions.

Hermann Schroeder (b Bernkastel, 1904). A composer who has a common ancestry with Beethoven.
Capriccetto for piano and violin. In "Georgii."

Hermann Unger (b Kamenz, Saxony, 1886; d Cologne, 1958)
Romanze for piano and violin. In "Georgii."

Ernest Walker (1870–1849) English
Variations on an Original Theme for piano, clarinet, and string trio. c1933. Written for Paul Wittgenstein.

FOR PIANO AND TAPE

William Dopmann
Distances from a Remembered Ground, 1982: Fantasy Variations on the Last Mazurka of Chopin; with offstage piano on tape. Newton Center, MA: Gunmar Music, 1985. Written for Leon Fleisher. 13 pp. NYPL.

Pozzi Escot
Interra II for piano left hand and tape (pre-recorded piano). Publications Contact International, 1980. Commissioned by John Felice. Dedicated to Basia. 8 movements.

FOR TWO LEFT HANDS

Clara Koehler-Heberlein
Polka-Mignonne, duet for 2 left hands. Philadelphia: T. Presser, 1911. E. NYPL.

Robert Phillips
Three Pieces for 2 left hands (at 2 pianos). New York: See-Saw Music Corp., 1973. Ms. *Chase; Nocturne for a Birthday; Hommage à Scriabin.* The first two pieces are simple, the third more difficult. Contemporary sound.

FOR TWO RIGHT HANDS

Franco Margola (b 1908) Italian
Sonata Pianistica per 2 mani destre (at 1 piano). Bongiovanni, 1969. I. *Con brio;* II. *Doloroso;* III. *Vivace.* Easier on two instruments, neo-classic, freely tonal. 10 min., 16 pp. M-D.

FOR THREE HANDS

Charles Valentin Alkan
13 Prières for piano 3 hands or pedal-piano, op. 64. Paris: Costallat & Co., n.d. The
upper part (hands) is fairly complex, the bass part (pedal) easy. 77 pp. L of C.

J. Beaujean
Das Erste Bach-Buch, für Gruppenunterricht und geselliges Spiel am Klavier. Hein-
richshofen, n.d. Very easy three-hand arrangements of two-hand music.

Theo Brand
Das Gassenbub und was Er elebt. Cologne: Hans Gerig, 1958. 7 short pieces. E.
Vogelhochzeit. Cologne: Hans Gerig, 1958. 7 short pieces.

John Clovis
The Last Five Minutes. New York: Mills Music, 1952. Very easy waltz for children.

Dietrich Erdmann
Thema und Variationen. Cologne: Hans Gerig Musikverlag, 1958. 5 simple variations;
teaching material.

Morton Feldman (b 1926). American, disciple of John Cage.
Piano (3 hands). New York: C.F. Peters, 1962. Dedicated to Lulla. Whole notes in a free
rhythm, atonal. E. L of C.

Karl Ludwig Traugott Gläser (1747–1798)
Sonata for 3 hands. New edition: Schott, Vermischte Handstücke.

Elliot Griffis (1893–1967) American
Tunes for 2, 3 and 4 Hands. New York: D.L. Schroeder. Most of these 53 short pieces in
folksong style are for 3 hands. Easy melody with harder accompaniment. Appealing, good for children. NYPL.

Mark Hambourg (b Boguchar 1879; d Cambridge, 1960). Russian-born, later a British
subject, he had an international playing career and formed a successful trio with his
brothers.
"Jesu, Joy of Man's Desiring": Chorale from Cantata No. 147, by J.S. Bach. London:
Oxford University Press, 1935. The melody (one-hand part) is elementary. L of C.

Johann Wilhelm Hässler (b Erfurt, 1747; d Moscow, 1822). German, successful in England and Russia.
Sonata for 3 hands. In "6 leichte Sonaten," Erfurt: 1786. New edition, Hanover: Nagels Musikarchiv No. 19, 1928. Written for the handicapped Countess Amalie zu Sachsen-Weimar. In one movement, C major, moderate. Early classical style similar to J.C. Bach. Good one-hand part. NYPL.

Paul Hoffer (1895–1949)
Kirmemusik (Church Music) for 3 hands. In "Georgii."

Mauricio Kagel (b Buenos Aires, 1931). Argentine composer and film maker.
Der Eid des Hippokrates (The Hippocratic Oath). Henry Litolff's Verlag, 1984. For 3 hands at 1 piano (2 or 3 players). An interesting concept: the upper part consists of one hand rhythmically striking the case of the piano, playing on the keyboard only at the very end. L of C.

Wilhelm Killmayer
Paradies (3 hands or 2 pianos), 1972. London: B. Schott, 1977. Contemporary style. 15 pp. M-E.

Kathryn Mishell (b Los Angeles). American pianist, composer, and author of a series of music for piano students.
Scherzo for 3 hands (1992). Written for pianist Danielle Martin during a period of temporary hand injury. Primo is "for either hand." Playful, scampering 6/8. 5 min. Both parts M-D. Available from the composer: 1406 Ridgecrest Drive, Austin, TX 78746.

Felix Petyrek (1892–1951)
Humoreske. In "Georgii."

Johann David Scheidler (b 1748; d Gotha, 1802). German cellist and composer.
Sonata for 3 hands.

Hermann Schroeder
Rondino. In "Georgii."

Robert Schumann (b Zwickau, 1810; d Endenich, near Bonn, 1856).
Abendlied, op. 85, no. 12. The last in the set of *Vierhändige Klavierstücke für kleine und grosse Kinder.* In Schumann's Works Vol. vi, 48; also in "Georgii."

Maria Szymanowska (b Warsaw, 1789; d St. Petersburg, 1831). Polish composer and widely traveled pianist.
Four Valses. Warsaw, 1822.

Alexander Tcherepnin, editor
Paraphrases on a Simple Theme ("Chopsticks," "Tati-Tati") by Borodin, Cui, Liadoff, Liszt, Rimsky-Korsakov and Stcherbatchev. In C.F. Peters Catalogue, European Publications: BEL 182.

W.M. Treloar
Sweet Childhood Waltz. Mexico, 1887. Easy upper part. L of C.

Hermann Zilcher (1881–1948)
Tanz-Caprice. In "Georgii."

FOR FIVE HANDS

Johann Friedrich Dalberg (b Herrnsheim, near Worms, 1760; d Aschaffenburg, 1812). Author, amateur composer, and aesthetician, one of the first German Romantics. Though physically deformed, he was a virtuoso pianist, and his writings cover such diverse subjects as meteorology and law.
Sonata for 5 hands, op. 19. Paris: N. Simrock, n.d. I. *Lento-Allegro;* II. *Menuetto* 1 and 2; III. *Prestissimo.* The left-hand page is the *secondo,* the right-hand page the *primo* plus a single-line treble part. Fairly simple classical style. L of C.

Maurice Ravel (1875–1937)
Frontispiece (1918). Paris: Salabert. For 5 hands at 2 pianos. Written as the frontispiece for a book of poetry by Ricciotto Canudo, reflecting that writer's combat experiences in World War I. 15 measures.

Theodore Edel is a pianist and Associate Professor and Artist-in-Residence in the Department of Performing Arts at the University of Illinois at Chicago. He has concertized in the former Soviet Union, England, and Italy on a Fulbright grant.